APPLYING THE GOSPEL

Suggestions for Christian Social Action in a Local Church

William M. Pinson, Jr.

BROADMAN PRESS
Nashville, Tennessee

Scripture quotations marked "TEV" are from *Today's English Version* of the New Testament. Copyright © American Bible Society 1966, 1971.

Dewey Decimal Classification: 361.7

Library of Congress Catalog Card Number: 75-8374

Printed in the United States of America

TO

BOBBIE

**Who applies the gospel daily
to the joy and benefit of all around her**

Preface

Many people contributed to the preparation of this book. Special appreciation is due the following:

Foy Valentine and the Christian Life Commission of the Southern Baptist Convention for making possible the travel and study necessary for research. The Home Mission Board of the Southern Baptist Convention for which I conducted a similar study on ministry resulting in the book *The Local Church in Ministry*, which contains some concepts in common with this book on *Applying the Gospel*.

The Southwestern Baptist Theological Seminary for a year's leave in which the major portion of the research and writing was done.

Mrs. Don Hammer and Mrs. Pauline Barnard for their capable typing of the various drafts of the manuscript.

The hundreds of persons who read and evaluated the original draft, making many helpful suggestions for changes.

Bobbie, my wife, and our daughters Meredith and Allison, for their encouragement and patience.

William M. Pinson, Jr.

Foreword

Applying the Gospel: Suggestions for Christian Social Action in a Local Church is a book that has been long in the making. The need for such a handbook is obvious. Yet the challenges met in preparing it have been formidable.

The challenge of finding a highly competent author was met when Dr. Pinson agreed to undertake the project.

The challenge of revising and improving the basic material was met when nearly a thousand concerned pastors, lay persons, and young people accepted a copy of the first draft of the manuscript with a view to offering constructive criticism of it.

The challenge of evaluating and coordinating the criticisms was met as various Southern Baptist agency and state Christian Life Commission representatives gave of their time and energy in furthering the process.

Then the challenge of producing and distributing what it was believed would be an immensely important and highly useful book was met when Dr. Charles A. Trentham as pastor, the deacons, and the First Baptist Church of Knoxville, Tennessee, designated for this purpose a major gift of extremely generous proportions from a bequest left to the church by Miss Vesta Jett; and then further generous contributions by Roy Rhodes, Mrs. Vester T. Hughes, Sr., and Vester T. Hughes, Jr., assured adequate funding for the completion of the project. The Christian Life Commission's earnest and sincere gratitude is hereby expressed to these donors for their significant gifts which represent unusual sensitivity and commitment to the mission of the church of Jesus Christ and which now make possible the distribution of this book to Southern Baptist pastors and lay leaders.

It is the Christian Life Commission's earnest hope and fervent prayer that this book with its "Suggestions for Christian Social Action" may be substantially helpful to Southern Baptists in *Applying the Gospel.*

Foy Valentine, *Executive Secretary*
Christian Life Commission
Southern Baptist Convention

Contents

Introduction

The world is plagued with unmet human need. Society is in crisis. The Bible sets forth a mandate to apply the good news of God to all of life. The Word of God and the plight of men call Christians to active social concern. Christians should take seriously the whole Bible. This calls for concern about salvation and starvation, repentance and racism, faith and family, regeneration and revolution, justification and justice, sanctification and sex, hell and housing, heaven and honesty, love and law—because the Bible includes insights and principles that relate to all of these.

With the Bible as our guide, Christians need to become as concerned about dirty air and water as we have been about dirty books and movies. We need to become as concerned about the immoral use of sex in marriage for irresponsible procreation as we have been about it apart from marriage in fornication. We need to become as concerned about people who are kept out of Baptist churches because of race as we have been about those let in without benefit of Baptist immersion. We need to become as concerned about what the poor have for supper as we have been about who is eligible to partake of the Lord's Supper. This we must do if we are true to the Bible.

Who Is This Book For?

Many churches and individual Christians are aware of the urgent need to apply their faith to daily life. They are eager to act. Others are awakening to their social responsibility in Christ. If you are among these concerned Christians, this book is designed to help you in Christian social action.

The following pages contain suggestions on how to relate the Christian faith to daily life. The approach is primarily for local Baptist congregations. Individuals, small groups, and non-church institutions can, of course, play significant roles in applying the gospel. Associations, state conventions, and other church-related organizations can be effective in Christian social action. This material should prove helpful to non-Baptists. Local Baptist churches, however, are the center of attention in this manual.

Churches differ too much for one program to be applicable to all of them. What kind of program a church develops will depend on its size, location, age, leadership, resources, and membership. The suggestions for application in this book must be adapted to each individual congregation.

Although this is directed primarily to pastors and other church staff members, it is for all church members. In most churches the pastor bears the main responsibility for programs. A congregation seldom rises above his leadership. On the other hand, without effective support by church members, no effort can succeed. Lay persons and staff leaders are equally important in an effective program of application.

How Is the Book Organized?

Organizationally, the first chapter of the book deals with the bases for a program of application. The Bible, the history of the Christian movement, and current needs each provides reasons why a church should have an emphasis on applied Christianity.

The second chapter sets forth general suggestions for developing a program of application.

Chapter III describes the steps to take in social action on specific issues.

The fourth chapter lists practical suggestions in each of the major areas of social concern.

Chapter V contains examples of application as carried out in churches of various types and sizes.

The sixth chapter is a list of resources which will be helpful to a church in carrying out a program of application.

What Do the Special Terms Mean?

In the book certain terms are used frequently: application, ethics, social change, social ministry, social action, social concern, social issues. In order to make the book more easily understood by persons not familiar with these terms, here is a brief definition of each.

"Application" is a term rather generally used by Southern Baptists for the function of a church in relating the gospel to social concerns. It means applying the Christian faith to daily life in areas such as family life, daily work, race relations, citizenship, and such special moral issues as alcohol and drug abuse, gambling, pornography, and poverty. Its primary concern is dealing with the causes of human hurt rather than ministering directly to persons who are hurt. Application is a kind of Christian love-at-a-distance.

"Ethics" is the study of oughtness in life—what a person or a society ought to be and do. Christian ethics sets forth oughtness in terms of God's revelation to man. It searches for answers to questions such as, "What does the Bible teach about family life?" "In the light of God's revelation in Christ, what ought I do about misunderstanding and hostility between persons of different races?" "As a Christian what should I do in support of responsible government?" Christian ethics deals with the way Christians should make decisions about social issues.

"Social ministry" is an effort to help persons in special need and those hurt by adverse social conditions, such as the poor, the neglected child, the sick, or the aging. It is an attempt to help those who are hurt rather than to deal with the social causes of their hurt.

"Social action" endeavors to correct harmful social conditions, such as war, an unjust and exploitative economic system, or a corrupt political system. It is distinguished from social ministry in that it is directed primarily to the social causes of human hurt rather than to the persons who are hurt.

"Social change" is the goal of social action. It refers to changes which come as a result of efforts to eliminate harmful, unjust social conditions such as pollution, organized crime, the open promotion of obscene literature and films, or grossly inadequate wages. Social change is the goal for which changed individuals work for God's glory and man's good. Social change is primarily concerned with altering social institutions, such as governments and economic systems.

"Social concern" is concern about society's problems which keep persons from being what God created them to be. It deals with human sin expressed through organized structures such as government, labor union, and business.

"Social issues" are significant subjects and problems in society. Unemployment, poverty, divorce, crime, traffic safety, pollution, population control, consumption of alcohol, drug abuse, hunger, gambling, racism, government, and pornography are examples of social issues.

"Mission Action" is defined both by the Brotherhood Commission and by Woman's Missionary Union as "the organized effort of a church to minister and to witness to persons of special need or circumstance." The Brotherhood Commission adds ". . . who, without this special effort, are often bypassed in the church's direct outreach activities." Woman's Missionary Union adds ". . . not members of the church or its programs."

How Can This Book Be Used?

A pastor and other members of the church staff may refer to it as they develop programs. Interested lay persons will find helpful suggestions here for applying Christian faith to life. Leaders of church organizations such as Sunday School, Church Training, Brotherhood, and Woman's Missionary Union may discover program ideas. The book could serve as the basis for a study in a deacons' retreat. It can be distributed to members of the church council and discussed. Church Training groups may use the book as a unit of study. College and seminary classes will find the material helpful in studying the role of churches in dealing with social problems.

In whatever ways the book is used, it is hoped that it will contribute to the advance of the cause of Christ. The motive for its publication is to glorify God and to meet the needs of men.

I
Bases for Application

The application of the gospel to life should be a major concern for Christians. Christians and churches should do something about issues such as divorce, slums, racism, alcohol, war, pollution, drugs, crime, poverty, obscene books and movies, and gambling. The bases for Christian social action are found in the Bible, in history, and in current needs.

The Biblical Mandate

The Bible is of central importance to the Christian. It records the unique self-disclosures of God. It provides the account of Jesus' life and teachings. It is the primary source, therefore, of finding how we are to live, who we ought to be, and what we ought to do. The Bible teaches that a Christian should apply the gospel to all of life. He should oppose anything that keeps persons from being what God created them to be. Most major biblical themes relate to the application of the Christian faith to daily life.

Nature and Will of God

According to the Bible, God created and sustains all that is. The world belongs to God. He is the sovereign Lord of the universe. He loves the world (John 3:16) and is in the process of bringing it to perfection (Rom. 8:19-22; Col. 1:20; Rev. 21:1-4). God's sphere of operation, therefore, is not simply the church or individual believers in Christ, but the whole world and all men. For his own redemptive purpose, he even works through those who do not believe in him (e.g. Rom. 13:1-5).

God makes his will known to us through his mighty acts in history and his commands and teachings. In the Old Testament scores of specific teachings call for social concern. Persons with special needs, such as the orphan, widow, poor, stranger, slave, divorcee, aged, sick, and hungry are to be cared for (e.g. Ex. 22:25-27; Lev. 14:21-32; Deut. 15:1-11; 24:1-4; Isa. 1:1-31; Amos 2:6; 5:11-12; 8:4-6). Many commands apply to social problems—drunkenness, crime, divorce, economic injustice, corruption in government, family breakdown, juvenile delinquency, prostitution, inadequate diet, abuse of the land, unsanitary living conditions, and sexual immorality (e.g. Lev. 18—19; Deut. 19—22; 24:1-4). God spoke through the Old Testament prophets to indicate his concern for every aspect of human life. These inspired men declared that God's primary concern was not religious ceremony or ritual, but acts of mercy, justice, and love (e.g. Jer. 5:25-29; Ex. 18; Hosea 6:6; Amos 5:21-24; Micah 6:6-8). They revealed God's great displeasure with those who corrupted society, oppressed the poor, waged cruel war, and ignored the plight of the powerless. Since we are children of our heavenly Father, we too must be concerned about all aspects of life.

Life and Teachings of Jesus

In the life and teachings of Jesus—the most complete revelation of God to man—the concern of God for total life is most clearly seen. Since believers are to live in accord with Jesus' life and teachings, they should also be concerned about every aspect of human life. Jesus' life and death were unique, and no one can or need repeat what he did. However, even the unique aspects of Jesus' life and death have bearing on the Christian's social concern.

In the incarnation, for example, God showed his interest in all facets of human life. Jesus was part of a family, worked as a carpenter, fulfilled citizenship responsibilities, and walked through the walls of prejudice and discrimination which separated people. He ministered to the poor and rich, the sick and well, the weak and strong, Gentile and Jew, old and young. He fed the hungry, healed the sick, forgave the sinner, comforted the sorrowing, accepted the outcast, and encouraged the downhearted. He "went about doing good" (Acts 10:38). Jesus demonstrated the way life ought to be lived.

The crucifixion reveals both the depth of man's depravity and the extent of God's love. In the light of the cross no one should take lightly the grip of sin on human life or expect quick, simple solutions to the complex issues of society. Coping with social problems demands sacrifice. The cross sets a pattern for the believer—voluntary sacrifice, in the will of God, motivated by love, to care for the total needs of men. Furthermore, through faith in Christ who died on the cross, we are set free from the guilt and power of sin to follow Christ's way. The cross liberated us for active concern for others.

The resurrection provides the Christian with assurance that ultimate victory belongs to God. Also the Christian knows that because of the resurrection, he does not struggle alone. As Paul put it, "I have been put to death with Christ on his cross, so that it is no longer I who live, but it is Christ who lives in me" (Gal. 2:19-20, TEV). A Christian cares for total human need because the Christ within him cares. A Christian struggles against the forces of evil not because he hopes to make a perfect world through such efforts but because it is the nature of Christ in him to oppose evil, establish justice, seek peace, and do good.

In the New Testament the second coming of Christ is related to application. Jesus indicated that when the Son of Man comes as King, one basis of judgment will be how men dealt with social needs (Matt. 25:31-46). Paul insisted that Christ's second coming was not to be used as an excuse for avoiding daily responsibilities in work and ministry (2 Thess. 3:5-14). Peter declared that godly living is called for by the fact of Christ's second coming (2 Pet. 3:10-14). James strongly united a belief in Christ's return with an insistence on good works (James 2:14-26; 5:7-8).

Jesus' mission was related to his role as Messiah. He announced his messiahship by reading a passage from Isaiah which expresses concern for applied religion:

> The Spirit of the Lord is upon me.
> He has anointed me to preach the Good News to the poor,
> He has sent me to proclaim liberty to the captives,
> And recovering of sight to the blind,
> To set free the oppressed,
> To announce the year when the Lord will save his people!
> (Luke 4:18-19, TEV)

This statement clearly refers to physical as well as spiritual needs. To the disciples of John the Baptist, Jesus offered as evidence of his messiahship his concern for total human need: "Go back and tell John what you are hearing and seeing: the blind can see, the lame can walk, the lepers are made clean, the deaf hear, the dead are raised to life, and the Good News is preached to the poor" (Matt. 11:4-5, TEV).

Jesus stated his mission in several different ways. He said that he had come "to seek and to save the lost" (Luke 19:10, TEV), to fulfill the Law and the Prophets (Matt. 5:17), "to serve and to give his life to redeem many people" (Mark 10:45, TEV), "in order that they might have life, life in all its fulness" (John 10:10, TEV). These statements indicate Jesus' concern for total human life. Such concern is also shown in his day-by-day ministry. As Luke stated it, Jesus "went everywhere, doing good and healing all who were under the power of the Devil" (Acts 10:38, TEV). His days were spent caring for total need—physical, spiritual, mental, and emotional. He took time to care for all types of persons (e.g. Matt. 9:9-10; 15:21-28; Mark 7:24-30; 10:13-14; Luke 7:1-17; 8:1-3; 18:35-43; 19:1-10; John 4:1-25, 46-53).

Jesus worked through organized effort as well as on a one-to-one basis. The few accounts in the New Testament of Jesus' organizing his followers are directly related to meeting human need. For example, Jesus sent out the disciples two by two with these instructions: "Whenever you go into a town and are made welcome, eat what is set before you, heal the sick in that town, and say to the people there, 'The Kingdom of God has come near you'" (Luke 10:8-9, TEV).

In ministering to human need Jesus often helped people to help themselves. He frequently restored persons to sound health which enabled them to earn their own way (e.g. Matt. 9:1-7,32-35; 11:5; 12:10-13; 15:30; 21:14; Mark 1:34, 40-42; 3:1-5; 8:22-26; Luke 7:22; John 5:1-9; 9:1-7). He also gave food to the needy (Matt. 14:16-21; 15:32-38; John 6:5-13), had his disciples carry a bag of money for the poor (John 13:29), and inspired men to give generously to care for the underprivileged (Luke 16:19-31; 18:18-22; 19:8). In other words, Jesus gave both a helping hand and a handout.

Jesus does not want us merely to deal with symptoms. A handout is not adequate. Baskets of food to the poor at Christmas, reading to the illiterate, taking children from the slums for a weekend in the country, for example, deal mainly with symptoms. On the other hand, job training and placement for the poor, literacy courses, and slum clearance projects, coupled with proclamation of the gospel, cope with more basic causes of human hurt. We should undertake social ministry such as providing help to individuals who are sick, hungry, jobless, illiterate, homeless, or aging. But we must not leave undone social action in Christ's name such as providing a combination of education and action to bring about changes in men's lives, in social structures, and in institutions.

Not only are Christians to follow the example of Jesus, they are also to obey his commandments and teachings. Jesus said, "If you love me, you will obey my commandments" (John 14:15, TEV). He also declared, "I have been given all authority in heaven and in earth. Go, then, to all peoples everywhere and make them my disciples: baptize them in the name of the Father and of the Son and of the Holy Spirit, and teach them to obey everything I have commanded you" (Matt. 28:18-20, TEV). Many of Jesus' commandments deal specifically with human relations and social issues.

Love is central in the teachings of Jesus. He indicated that the whole Law of Moses and the teachings of the prophets depend on the commands to love God and to love your neighbor as you love yourself (Matt. 22:37-40). Jesus made clear that love for neighbor is to be no mild virtue or mere sentiment of vague goodwill. As the parable of the good Samaritan shows, love calls for action to care for the needs of anyone who hurts.

In a simple society such needs can often be cared for on an informal, personal basis. If a man's house burns, his neighbors can help build another. If a man is ill and cannot harvest his crops, his neighbors can harvest them for him. A volunteer fire department can control fires. Sunday School classes or Baptist Men's units can help clothe and feed poor families. The demands of love are obvious and more easily met when society is relatively uncomplicated.

In a complex urban society, however, the demands of love are often complicated. The problems related to block after block of substandard housing are not easily remedied. The needs of thousands of poor people crowded into rat-infested slums are not easily met. Millions of aging, handicapped, sick persons call for more help than a minority of committed people in churches can give. Industrial and municipal pollution, war, graft, price fixing, and unjust tax structures cannot be dealt with effectively by the men's Sunday School class working alone. Individuals on a personal basis should help those who have been injured or have needs. But the kind of love Jesus commanded calls also for group action. Christian love demands a united expression through the channels of government, schools, businesses, churches, and denominational programs.

Tutoring slow learners can be an act of love by a Christian; so can political action to improve a school system or to provide adequate annual income to undergird more stable homes for children. Repairing a house for a poor family can be an act of love by a church group; so also can efforts by Christians through business and government to provide adequate housing for millions of low-income families. An antilitter campaign by a church youth group can be a Christian ministry to curtail a source of pollution; so also can political action by Christians to reduce air, water, and noise pollution by individuals, business, or government. In our day Christians must love corporately as well as personally, if we are to love effectively.

Servanthood is a basic theme in Jesus' teachings. It is closely related to love. Jesus stressed that his disciples are to serve, not to be served. He declared, "For even the Son of Man did not come to be served; he came to serve and to give his life to redeem many people" (Mark 10:45, TEV). As servants, individual Christians are to search for ways to help care for the total needs of persons. A church as a group of believers is also to function as a servant. A church does not exist to be served by a community but to serve a community in Christ's name.

Judgment, according to Jesus, is related to social concern. Jesus said: "When the Son of man shall come in his glory, and all the holy angels with him, then shall he sit upon the throne of his glory: And before him shall be gathered all nations; and he shall separate them one from another, as a shepherd divideth his sheep from the goats: And he shall set the sheep on his right hand, but the goats on the left. Then shall the King say unto them on his right hand, Come, ye blessed of my

Father, inherit the kingdom prepared for you from the foundation of the world: For I was an hungered, and ye gave me meat: I was thirsty, and ye gave me drink: I was a stranger, and ye took me in: Naked, and ye clothed me: I was sick, and ye visited me: I was in prison, and ye came unto me. Then shall the righteous answer him, saying, Lord, when saw we thee an hungered, and fed thee? or thirsty, and gave thee drink? When saw we thee a stranger, and took thee in? or naked, and clothed thee? Or when saw we thee sick, or in prison, and came unto thee? And the King shall answer and say unto them, Verily I say unto you, Inasmuch as ye have done it unto one of the least of these my brethren, ye have done it unto me. Then shall he say also unto them on the left hand, Depart from me, ye cursed, into everlasting fire, prepared for the devil and his angels: For I was an hungered, and ye gave me no meat: I was thirsty, and ye gave me no drink: I was a stranger, and ye took me not in: naked, and ye clothed me not: sick, and in prison, and ye visited me not. Then shall they also answer him, saying, Lord, when saw we thee an hungered, or athirst, or a stranger, or naked, or sick, or in prison, and did not minister unto thee? Then shall he answer them, saying, Verily I say unto you, Inasmuch as ye did it not to one of the least of these, ye did it not to me. And these shall go away into everlasting punishment: but the righteous into life eternal" (Matt. 25:31-46, KJV).

One way to care for some of the needs Jesus mentioned is to work to prevent them from developing. Prevention is better than correction. Striving to curtail crime and delinquency is as important, for example, as visiting those in prison. Working to improve race relations is really more vital than helping clean up the debris after a race riot. Laboring to eliminate economic injustice is as significant as distributing food and clothes to the unemployed or underpaid.

The kingdom of God is central in Jesus' teachings. Jesus did not define the kingdom. He described it. The kingdom essentially is the reign of God in human life. Those in the kingdom do the will of God. The kingdom is both a present reality and a future hope. God both establishes his reign and calls on men to help extend it. As members of the kingdom of God, Christians are to follow the rule of God in all aspects of life. Pious talk is an inadequate response to the King;

doing his will is required (Matt. 7:21-23). Christians are to pray and
work for God's will to be done on earth as it is in heaven (Matt. 6:10).
God's will is to be done in all areas of life, social as well as personal.
This includes family life, race relations, daily work, citizenship responsibilities, and international affairs.

Other teachings of Jesus show the importance of Christian social
concern. Jesus warned of greed that choked compassion for those in
need (Luke 16:19-31). He insisted that protecting the powerless is as
important as prayer (Matt. 23:14). He declared that it was wrong to
pay careful attention to religious rules and ritual while ignoring justice,
mercy, and honesty (Matt. 23:23). He taught that rules for religious
observance should not stand in the way of ministering to human need
(Matt. 12:9-14). He praised Zacchaeus for his plans to give half his
belongings to the poor (Luke 19:8-9). Jesus also spoke concerning social
institutions such as family, business, and government. And he dealt with
specific issues such as divorce (Matt. 5:31-32; 19:3-9; Mark 10:2-12;
Luke 16:18), taxation (Matt. 22:15-22; Mark 12:13-17; Luke 20:19-26),
and materialism (Matt. 6:19-34; 13:22; Luke 12:13-34). The Christian
is obligated to concern himself with these social issues which concerned
Jesus.

The Ministry of the Holy Spirit

The ministry of the Holy Spirit is closely related to Christian social
concern. In the early church the Holy Spirit helped break down the
barriers of prejudice which separated Christians from one another. The
book of Acts is a record of the acts of the Spirit, part of which shows
that God cares for all persons without respect of race or nationality
or class. Jesus promised the power of the Spirit would enable the
disciples to be witnesses unto him in all parts of the earth (Acts 1:8).
At Pentecost the Holy Spirit came upon persons without distinction
as to race or nationality (Acts 2:1-11). The Holy Spirit showed his
concern for Samaritans (Acts 8:4-17), black persons (Acts 8:27-31),
Roman soldiers (Acts 10:17-23,44-48), and other Gentiles. Those filled
with the Spirit were cleansed from prejudice and unjust discrimination.
Spirit-filled persons will be so cleansed today.

Jesus indicated the Holy Spirit would reveal truth to Christians (John

16:13-15,25-26). That is a comforting promise for those grappling with the complexities of modern social problems. Paul testified that the Spirit helped Christians to see the truth and to do it (1 Cor. 2:12-15). Acts records how the Holy Spirit guided the early Christians (Acts 8:27-31; 10:17-20; 16:6; 20:22-23). On the basis of his own experiences Paul urged believers to let the Holy Spirit direct them (Gal. 5:16-25). Surrounded by difficult choices in regard to social problems the Christian ought to exercise all his own resources in deciding what to do. But he should also be sensitive to the leadership of the Holy Spirit.

Often a Christian's failure to deal with social injustice is due not to lack of knowledge but to a sense of powerlessness. A believer may feel powerless in the face of vast needs and gigantic problems. His own sense of inadequacy paralyzes him. The Christian's source of power for bearing a faithful witness is the Holy Spirit (Acts 1:8). John assures us that the Holy Spirit is more powerful than any adversary we face (1 John 4:4). When we are so perplexed that we don't even know how to pray, the Spirit helps us (Rom. 8:26). The Holy Spirit will empower us to *do* the truth he has led us to understand. He equips us with the gifts necessary for our task (1 Cor. 12:4-11). And when we experience setback and hurt, he comforts us. The Spirit assures us that no matter what happens, we are indeed the children of God (Rom. 8:14-16).

The Christian Life

God created man in his own image. Whatever else the image of God may mean, it certainly means that insofar as our human limitations permit we are to be like God. But all men sin and fall short of God's will. The result of sin is sorrow and death. All sin is ultimately against God. Sin also affects individuals, personal relations, and society. The Bible indicates that sin is expressed in many ways, such as injustice, oppression of the poor, apathy in the face of human need, greed, dishonesty in business, cruelty, failure to care for the needs of the fatherless and widows in their weakness, murder, adultery, theft, false oaths, and corruption in government. These are against God's will. They are the consequence of man's self-centeredness. They all result in suffering and threaten the stability of society.

God provides a way to abundant and eternal life for sinners through

Jesus Christ. "For sin pays its wage—death; but God's free gift is eternal life in union with Christ Jesus our Lord" (Rom. 6:23, TEV). God's grace makes possible man's response of faith and obedience to his Son. "For it is by God's grace that you have been saved, through faith. It is not your own doing, but God's gift. There is nothing here to boast of, since it is not the result of your own efforts. God is our Maker, and in our union with Christ Jesus he has created us for a life of good works, which he has already prepared for us to do" (Eph. 2:8-10, TEV).

The Bible makes it quite clear that salvation is to affect a person's total life. "If any man be in Christ, he is a new creature: old things are passed away; behold, all things are become new" (2 Cor. 5:17). God's desire is not simply to redeem a person's soul but also to transform all his life. God's concern is all of life, not simply religion. Living the Christian life, therefore, involves not only praying, tithing, and worshiping but also loving others, caring for the needy, and giving of self in applying the good news to correct social problems.

A Christian is not only to believe but also to behave according to God's will. Faith and works go together. The faith that is part of salvation leads to works of love in obedience to God's will (James 1:27; 2:15-16). The person who truly loves God will love his fellowman (1 John 4:19-21). And the love which is implanted by God in the Christian is not to be expressed just in words, "It must be true love, which shows itself in action" (1 John 3:18, TEV). Just as sin has a social dimension, so does salvation.

The basic pattern for the Christian life is the character of God as revealed in his Son, Jesus Christ. According to the Bible, the child of God is to be becoming like his heavenly Father. The Old Testament clearly sets forth the challenge to be like God. For example, in Leviticus God is recorded as declaring, "Ye shall be holy: for I the Lord your God am holy" (Lev. 19:2). Throughout the Old Testament the standard for human conduct is divine conduct: God is holy; men are to be holy. God is just; men are to be just. God is merciful; men are to be merciful. In the New Testament the call to be like God is sounded even more clearly. Jesus said, "You must be perfect—just as your Father in Heaven is perfect" (Matt. 5:48, TEV). And Paul wrote, "Since you are God's dear children, you must try to be like him" (Eph. 5:1, TEV).

What does it mean for men to be like God? The answer is found basically in Jesus Christ. Philip requested Jesus, "Show us the Father" (John 14:9, TEV). Jesus replied, "If you have seen me you have seen the Father." God was in Christ. Jesus put it, "I am in the Father and the Father is in me" (John 14:11, TEV). In various ways the New Testament stresses that in Jesus we can see what it means to be like God, to live in the will of God (e.g. John 1:1-5,14-15; 10:30,38; 14:8-10,15; 15:12-17; 17:21; Col. 1:15-19; 2:8).

In a sense, therefore, the Christian is to become like Jesus. Jesus frequently called men to follow him and to be like him (e.g. Matt. 11:29; Mark 8:34; John 13:34). New Testament writers often stress that Christians are to follow the example of Jesus (e.g. Rom. 15:5; Gal. 3:27; Eph. 5:1; 1 John 2:6; 3:3,7; 4:17). John wrote, "He who says that he lives in God should live just as Jesus Christ did" (1 John 2:6, TEV).

In Christ's life, the believer sees the "way" that he is to walk, the pattern for his life. Through personal faith in Christ who died on the cross the believer is set free to follow Christ's way. The indwelling of the risen Christ (Gal. 2:20) and the presence of the Holy Spirit (John 16:13-15; Acts 1:8; 1 Cor. 6:19-20; Eph. 3:16; 6:17) enable the Christian to follow Christ's way. And the promise of Jesus' coming again encourages the believer to keep on following his way in spite of how difficult it becomes.

Many reasons are given in the Bible why Christians should obey God by applying their faith to daily life. As Christians we are to obey God because of who he is—the Lord—and because of what he has done for us. We are to love one another because he has forgiven us in Christ (Eph. 4:32). We are to conduct ourselves in a manner worthy of the gospel (Phil. 1:27) and as a witness to unbelievers (1 Peter 2:15; 3:1-3). Christians are also warned that wrong actions result in punishment and that right conduct brings reward (e.g. Matt. 7:24-27; 25:31-46). The indwelling Christ through the Holy Spirit aids the believer in faithfully following God's will in all of the Christian life (John 14:15-17,25-26; Gal. 2:20; Phil. 4:13).

Church

Individual Christians are clearly called to be like God in concern
for total life. And since Jesus Christ is the most complete revelation
of God, we are to follow his steps and obey his teachings. But the
Christian life is not a purely personal affair. The church is the corporate
expression of life in Christ. Much of the Bible's teaching about the
nature and function of a church is related to the application of the
gospel to daily life. As the "people of God" the church is to be concerned
about all the aspects of life which God is concerned about. As "the
body of Christ" a church is to function much as Christ functioned.
According to the New Testament, a church's basic function is to bear
witness to what God has done through Jesus Christ. All other functions
relate to this primary task. The Bible sets forth at least these basic
ways a church bears witness: fellowship, proclamation, ministry, and
application.

Fellowship is the practice of love and concern by those who share
a common allegiance to Christ as Lord. Forgiving and accepting one
another, breaking down walls of race and class which separate believers,
praying for each other, strengthening one another, restoring one another,
and sharing material possessions were some of the ways the early
believers expressed love and concern. The Christian community is to
be a colony of the new heaven and new earth which God will one
day bring to consummation. As such it is to be inclusive, welcoming
persons from all races, economic levels, and social backgrounds (e.g.
Acts 5:15-16; 8:4-7,26-40; 10:1-8,34-35; Rom. 1:14).

Proclamation is the verbal expression of the gospel. Proclamation
is essential; apart from telling the "good news" about Jesus Christ,
men cannot be saved (Rom. 10:14-17). The command of Jesus is to
go into all the world preaching the gospel, baptizing, making disciples
(Matt. 28:16-20; Acts 1:8). The earliest Christians carried out Jesus'
injunction. They told all kinds of people from every walk of life about
new life in Christ. The book of Acts is the story of how ethnic and
geographical walls were scaled by the first-century believers as they
went throughout the world talking about salvation in Christ.

Ministry is a demonstration of the concern of Christians for the total

needs of persons. Ministry is love in action. It involves caring for weak, ✓
hurt, or disadvantaged people. The ministry of the early churches, like
that of Jesus, was to the total needs of all kinds of people (e.g. Acts
3:1-10; 9:32-35; 14:8-10; 16:16-19; 2 Cor. 1:4).

Application is the relating of the Christian gospel to social concerns. ✓
It is bringing God's good news to bear on the issues of daily life. It
is Christian social concern that issues in Christian social action related
to family life, daily work, race relations, citizenship, and special moral
concerns such as alcohol and drug abuse, gambling, and pornography.
It is Christian involvement to drain the swamps of corruption and
injustice to prevent the mosquitoes of crime and violence from breeding.
As the early churches involved themselves in application, they served
as God's salt, God's light, and God's leaven to permeate the structures
and institutions of society. By so doing, they effected change for God
and for good with regard to such social evils as child exposure, the
status of inferiority accorded to women, sex abuse, and human slavery.

All of these are interrelated. Fellowship, ministry, and application,
for example, authenticate proclamation and can win a hearing which
might not otherwise be given. Worship and Christian education also
contribute to the witness of the church. They are support functions
and assist the people of God in carrying out their primary witness
tasks.

Examples of Specific Biblical Teachings on Social Issues [1]

Teachings about God, Jesus, the Christian life, and the church support
the application of the gospel to life. In addition, the Bible sets forth
specific teachings about personal morality, interpersonal relations, social
institutions, and social issues. These teachings show God's concern for
all of life and serve as a basis for an emphasis on application. What
God clearly teaches in his Word should certainly be of concern to
Christians. The following paragraphs are not intended to present proof
texts for biblical teachings on specific issues. Rather they are intended
to demonstrate God's concern for social issues and problems. The Bible
sets forth God's ideal for human life. When people fail to live up to

---

[1] Adaptation of material used in article on the Bible and ethics in volume 12 of *The Broadman Bible Commentary* (Nashville: Broadman Press, 1971).

the ideal, however, provision is made by God for forgiveness. Christians are to minister to the needs of those who fall short of God's ideal.

Individual.—Much of the Bible's teaching is concerned with the individual—with his health, well-being, attitudes, and personal conduct. Large portions of the Old Testament law are devoted to health measures. Diet and sanitation are emphasized (e.g. Lev. 11—15). The New Testament teachings on health are less extensive, but they are no less significant. The Christian is to care for his body primarily because it belongs to God (1 Cor. 6:13). It is to be a living sacrifice (Rom. 12:1), and it is the temple of the Holy Spirit (1 Cor. 6:19). The individual's mental and emotional well-being are also of concern to God. The Christian is to have the mind of Christ and to set his mind on things above (Phil. 2:5; Col. 3:2). He is to rejoice, be filled with hope, trust in God, reject anxiety, and let the peace of Christ rule in his heart (Matt. 6:25-34; John 14:27; Rom. 15:13; Phil. 3:1; Col. 3:15; 1 Tim. 4:10). Virtues to be cultivated and vices to be eliminated are emphasized in the Bible (e.g., Psalms 1; 15; 24; Job 31; Ezekiel 18; Gal. 5:16-25; Eph. 4:1 to 5:20; Col. 3:1-17; 2 Cor. 12:19-21; 1 Tim. 6:1-21; 2 Tim. 3:1-15; Titus 2:1 to 3:11; 2 Peter 1:3-11).

Interpersonal Relations.—Many of the virtues and vices discussed in the Bible apply not only to individuals but also to relations between individuals. In the Old Testament law, much attention is paid to interpersonal relations. The Ten Commandments indicate that each person's rights are to be respected. A person is not to take away another's life, wife, property, or good name—or even ponder such an act (Ex. 20:13-17). The Bible declares that persons in need are to be cared for and that social structures which harm people are to be corrected. The demands of love include justice in the social order. The Old Testament law makes special provision for the poor and the powerless (e.g. Ex. 22:25-27; Lev. 14:21-32; Deut. 15:1-11). The prophets called for both individuals and the nation to care for the poor, the widows, the orphans, and others in need. They prophesied God's judgment on those who did not seek justice for the oppressed (e.g. Isa. 1:1-31; Amos 2:6; 5:11-12; 8:4-6). Jesus taught that his disciples were to love, forgive, and minister to others. New Testament writers stressed bearing one another's burdens (Gal. 6:2), doing good to all men (Gal. 6:10), helping the weak (1 Thess.

5:14; James 1:27), and caring for persons in need (1 John 3:17-18).

Race.—The Bible teaches that all men are to be treated with dignity and respect regardless of race, nationality, religion, or social standing. All men are created in the image of God (Gen. 1:26-27). God loves all men and provides for the unjust as well as the just (Matt. 5:45). Christ died for all men (Rom. 5:18). God is no respecter of persons (Acts 10:34). In spite of efforts to justify racial discrimination and segregation on the basis of the Bible, no adequate exegesis supports such interpretations. Rather, biblical principles and teachings make a strong case against prejudice, unjust discrimination, and racial segregation with its inevitable implication of racial inferiority. The Bible calls for love and justice to guide relations between persons of different races, nations, and ethnic groups.

Family Life.—The Bible teaches that marriage is a union of male and female (Gen. 2:24). Marriage has been established and blessed by God (Gen. 1:27-28; 2:18-24) and is honorable (Heb. 13:4). Those with a gift for celibacy may refrain from marriage in order to devote themselves more fully to service in the kingdom of God (Matt. 19:10-12; 1 Cor. 7:7,25-27), but celibacy in and of itself is not more pleasing to God than marriage.

Marriage is to be an exclusive union between one man and one woman (Matt. 19:4-6; 1 Cor. 7:10; 1 Tim. 3:2,12). There is to be no adultery, polygamy, homosexuality, or continued dependence on parents. The union is to last a lifetime (1 Cor. 7:39). Divorce, Jesus indicated, was not part of God's original plan for marriage (Matt. 19:3-12). The New Testament possibly allows divorce and remarriage in the case of sexual infidelity or desertion by an unbelieving mate (Matt. 5:31-32; 19:3-12; 1 Cor. 7:15. Mark 10:2-12 and Luke 16:18 do not provide any grounds for divorce and remarriage).

The Bible teaches that one purpose of God for marriage is to provide intimate companionship for a man and woman (Gen. 2:18,22; Matt. 19:4-6). Another related purpose is to provide a constructive expression of sexuality (1 Cor. 7:2-6; Heb. 13:4). The Bible views sex as a good gift from God which can bring happiness when used in the way God intended. The Bible states that sexual intercourse, an expression of the one flesh union (Gen. 2:24), is only for a man and woman married to each other. Homosexuality, incest, and bestiality as well as fornication and adultery are forbidden (Ex. 20:14; Lev. 18:6-23; 20:10-21; Matt. 5:27-30; 19:9,18; Rom. 1:26-27; 1 Cor. 5:1; 6:9-10,15-20; Rev. 21:8). Human sexuality exists apart from marriage, of course. Since marriage is not God's will for everyone, Christians should seek to help the never-married, the widowed, and the divorced to find expressions of their sexuality in line with Christian insights and the mind of Christ. Another purpose of God for marriage is reproduction (Gen. 1:28). However, the Bible does not indicate that procreation should be an intended aspect of every act of sexual intercourse (1 Cor. 7:1-5). Conception control when practiced for worthy reasons does not violate biblical teachings. In light of the problems caused by the population explosion it may well be a Christian obligation. Still another purpose of God for marriage is the nurture provided in the home for the young and the old. This affectionate nurture is indispensable for personal and social well-being.

The Bible sets forth guidelines for family relations. Between husband and wife the key terms are love, fidelity, respect, and consideration for each other's needs (Eph. 5:21-33; Col. 3:18-19; 1 Cor. 7:1-5). Children are to obey and honor their parents (Deut. 5:16; Eph. 6:1-4; Col. 3:20). Parents are to love, discipline, nurture, and provide for the physical needs of their children; they are not to provoke them to anger; and they are to give them religious instruction (Ex. 12:26-27; Deut. 6:2; Eph. 6:4; Col. 3:21; 1 Tim. 5:8; Titus 2:4).

Economics and Daily Work.—The Bible contains no blueprint for an economic system, but it does contain guidelines for economic activity. The Old Testament sets forth many rules relating to such things as harvesting crops, lending money, and owning land (e.g. Ex. 22:1-14; Lev. 19; Deut. 19—22). Private ownership of property is recognized in the Bible, but ownership is never considered absolute (e.g. Lev. 19:9-10; 25:23). The land and all that is on it belong to God (Ex. 19:5; Deut. 10:14; Job 41:11; Ps. 24:1, Isa. 66:2). Man is a steward and is obligated not to abuse or pollute God's land.

God gives the power to gain wealth (Deut. 8:17-18); no one is a "self-made man." Wealth is to be gained by honest labor, not by theft, dishonesty, or oppressive tactics (Prov. 21:6; Mark 7:21; 12:40; Luke

19:2-10; Eph. 4:28). In both the Old Testament and New Testament it is recognized that the poor are to be provided for and not taken advantage of (e.g. Job 31:16-22; Isa. 58:7-8; Amos 2:6-7; 4:1-3; 5:12-13; 8:4-6; Matt. 25:31-46; Luke 14:12-14).

The New Testament contains strong warnings about the danger of wealth. Wealth can be an obstacle to entering into the kingdom of God (Matt. 19:23-24). It is deceitful, creating a false sense of security (Luke 12:16-21). The love of money is the root of all kinds of evil (1 Tim. 6:9-10). Material treasures are not as valuable as spiritual ones (Matt. 6:19-21). Concern for material possessions can choke spiritual growth (Matt. 13:22; Mark 4:19); therefore, men should not be anxious about material things (Matt. 6:24-34; Luke 12:22-30; 14:28-33). Giving undue respect to the wealthy can disrupt Christian fellowship (James 2:1-9). Corrupt and ill-gained wealth will bring the stern judgment of God (James 5:1-6).

Paul taught that a person is to work to earn a living (1 Thess. 4:11; 2 Thess. 3:10). If for some reason a person is unable to work, he should be cared for. Income from work is to be used to provide for one's family (Matt. 7:11; 15:1-6; 1 Tim. 5:8), to contribute to the support of those who preach the gospel (1 Cor. 9:14), to care for the poor (Eph. 4:28; James 1:27), to pay taxes (Rom. 13:6-7), and to provide for persons in special need (Rom. 12:8,13,20; 2 Cor. 8:1-5). Paul taught that the Christian's basic calling is to live "in Christ," and that work is one aspect of that calling (1 Cor. 7:20; Eph. 4:4).

Citizenship.—The Bible provides no guidelines for a particular form of government. It does indicate, however, something about the nature of government and of the responsibility of citizens. The Bible recognizes government as a valid institution. Jesus accepted government, operated within its framework, acknowledged government's right of taxation, and submitted to its authority (Matt. 17:24-25; 22:15-22; Mark 12:17). Paul taught that government is ordained of God and exists to protect those who do right, to punish those who do wrong, and to promote the welfare of the citizens (Rom. 13:1-7).

The Bible indicates that government officials should be men of upright character who will carry out the legitimate functions of the state. They should be honest and accept no bribes (e.g. Ex. 23:8; Isa. 1:23). They should fear God and keep his commandments (Deut. 17:16-20; Ps. 2:11). They should recognize that their authority comes from God (Mark 10:42-43; John 19:11; Rom. 13). They should not get drunk (Prov. 31:4-5), act unjustly, or show favoritism (Lev. 19:15; Deut. 16:19). Jesus and the prophets were severely critical of government leaders who abused their position (2 Sam. 12:1-10; Isa. 1:23; Amos 5:7,12; Mark 8:15; Luke 13:32).

According to the New Testament, Christians are to honor government officials (Rom. 13:7; 1 Pet. 2:17), pay taxes (Matt. 22:21; Rom. 13:6-7), obey laws (Rom. 13:1-7), and pray for officials (1 Tim. 2:1-2). They must use moral discernment in their support of civil government, however, and are not to submit to the state when to do so would be contrary to God's will (Acts 5:29).

War and military force are frequently dealt with in the Bible. The ideal of God is peace (Ps. 46:9; Isa. 2:4; 11:1-10; Micah 4:2-5; 1 Chron. 28:2-3); and the horror of war is realistically presented (2 Sam 2:23; Ps. 79:1-3; Jer. 4:19; 16:4; Isa. 1:1-10). Yet the Old Testament pictures God as sometimes allowing, even commanding, war (Lev. 26:7-8; Deut. 7:1-2; 20:1-20; 2 Sam. 22:35; 1 Chron. 5:22). Some of Jesus' actions and teachings as recorded in the New Testament have been used to approve war. For example, he taught that wars and rumors of wars would persist but would not necessarily indicate his return (Matt. 24:6). He accepted military men (Luke 14:31) and praised the faith of one (Luke 7:1-9). Other teachings of Jesus are used to support pacifism. Jesus praised peacemakers (Matt. 5:9) and called for his disciples to love their enemies, practice non-resistance, and do good to those who harmed them (Matt. 5:38-48). He taught that those who live by the sword will die by the sword and commanded Peter to put up his weapon (Matt. 26:52).

The New Testament is practically silent, except in terms of principles, on such issues as Christian participation in political action and church-state relations. Direct Christian political action, apart from revolution, was hardly a live option for most early Christians under the Roman dictatorship. Yet it must be assumed that responsible Christian citizenship in a democracy calls for involvement in political action. Biblical insight and historical evidence strongly support separation as the best relationship between church and state. Separation, however, does not mean that Christians must refrain from political involvement and political action.

Historical Precedents

Throughout the history of the Christian movement, churches and individuals have taken seriously the biblical mandate to apply faith to life. In word and action they have struggled to bring practice into line with profession. Their efforts do not provide an authoritative basis for application of the gospel to life. The Bible provides this. But their emphasis on application does demonstrate that social concern has been a consistent part of the mainstream of the Christian movement.

Early Churches

The early churches stressed the biblical standards for family life, daily work, citizenship, and solutions for special moral problems such as alcoholism and usury. They also cared for those in need, such as orphans, widows, the sick, and the poor. Churches and individual Christians had an influence on family life, amusements, politics, sexual practices, economics, race relations, class conflicts, poverty, and other social issues. The churches, however, affected social structures very little in the first decades of the Christian movement. There were several reasons for this: Christians were a very small part of the population and could make little direct impact on social institutions. Christians for the most part came from the powerless classes of society and had little direct influence on the politically, economically, and socially powerful. The early churches concentrated their efforts on establishing a beachhead in the pagan world. Many Christians expected the immediate return of Christ and saw no need for trying to improve a social order which they thought was soon to be destroyed.

Soon the circumstances for Christian action in society altered. Christians became more numerous. Persons from the ruling classes were converted. Established churches grew strong enough to exert influence on society. It became apparent that the coming again of Christ might be a more distant event than some had thought, and Christians began to turn their attention more to bringing God's will to bear on the present order. Spokesmen and writers such as Justin Martyr, Origen, Tertullian, Chrysostom, and Augustine set forth the claims of Christ on all aspects of life. They dealt with problems and issues such as war, slavery, church-state relations, abortion, divorce, delinquency, daily work, materialism, and recreation. At first, attention was given mainly to what Christians should do about these issues. But soon efforts were made to present God's demands for all men and for the institutions of society.

Middle Ages

In the fourth century Christianity became the established state religion of the Roman Empire. Churches began to exert great influence on society. At the same time society also influenced the churches. As the churches became worldly powers, they lost much of their spiritual zeal. This is a danger we must guard against today. However, the churches in the Middle Ages helped to hold a disintegrating society together. Churchmen assumed many responsibilities once performed by the state. In some places government, education, welfare, and the courts came under control of church leaders.

During the Middle Ages elaborate schemes were worked out by church leaders for government, economics, family life, and war. In spite of corruption, unbiblical doctrines, and numerous deplorable practices, many churchmen continued to apply the Christian faith to life. Churches did not completely ignore the fact that being a Christian called for more than religious ritual.

Reformation

The leaders of the Protestant Reformation, such as Martin Luther, John Calvin, and John Knox, were concerned about both the application and the proclamation of the gospel. They were involved in political and economic action to try to make a more just society. They preached and wrote concerning social institutions and moral problems. They gave their attention to such practical subjects as the form and function of the state, war, civil disobedience, usury, daily work, economics, marriage, sex, divorce, crime and punishment, amusements, and Christian responsibility for the social order.

Modern Period

All major Christian spokesmen during the past three hundred years have devoted much attention to the application of the Christian faith to daily life. They have been concerned about social problems and have worked for justice in the social order. Almost without exception this has been true of outstanding preachers, both pastors and evangelists, and theological writers.[2] Laymen have been particularly involved in applying the gospel to daily life and social issues.

John Wesley fought the slave trade, beverage alcohol, and abuse of the poor. William Wilberforce, an English layman, labored successfully in Parliament for the abolition of slavery. Timothy Dwight, while president of Yale, worked for women's rights and against racial discrimination in eighteenth-century New England. Henry Ward Beecher, as a pastor, preached against slavery and supported the Abolitionist cause in England during the Civil War. Charles Spurgeon in London dealt vigorously and courageously with issues such as slavery, war, unjust labor conditions, and poverty. Charles Finney, famous nineteenth-century evangelist, worked for the abolition of slavery and aided the underground railroad. Billy Sunday preached against alcohol and the oppression of the poor by the rich. Woodrow Wilson, a Presbyterian layman, especially endeavored to relate his faith to the realm of government. And Billy Graham has frequently preached and written on many social problems.[3]

Organized religion has played a key role in social change in America. Ministers and laymen helped fan the flames of revolution in colonial America. Baptists and others waged an active political campaign to get constitutional guarantees for religious liberty and separation of church and state. Numerous church groups enthusiastically supported the Abolitionist cause prior to the Civil War. The Civil War and World War I were looked upon by many church leaders as holy crusades. The role of the churches in the struggle for economic justice and labor

---

[2] See Clyde E. Fant, Jr. and William M. Pinson, Jr., *20 Centuries of Great Preaching.* Waco, Texas: Word Books, 1971. See also David Moberg, *The Great Reversal* (Philadelphia: J. B. Lippincott Co., 1972) for a discussion of why many conservative Christians turned away from social action in the early part of the twentieth century.

[3] See David Lockard's *The Unheard Billy Graham.* (Waco, Texas: Word Books, 1970).

reforms must not be overlooked. Churches campaigned successfully for
Prohibition. More recently the civil rights movement was largely an
outgrowth of the efforts of churchmen and churches.

On a local level, churches have often been involved in social action.
Crusades against gambling, pornography, alcohol, and obscene movies
have been common. Others have dealt actively with drug abuse, housing,
political corruption, crime, civil rights, delinquency, labor-management
relations, hunger, poverty, pollution, planned parenthood, and war. Such
efforts have involved persons from a variety of denominations and
theological camps.

A Christian or a church indifferent to the application of the gospel
to life is out of step with the finest Christian leaders throughout the
history of the Christian movement. Those who have given themselves
most completely to Christ have related faith to all of life. Their views
on specific issues may not always have been correct. But at least they
endeavored to apply the gospel to the problems of their time. They
refused to heed the warning, "Play it safe. Don't rock the boat." Rather
they preferred to follow the example of Christ and the early church.

Contemporary Needs

Contemporary needs form another basis for application. The need
for the application of the gospel and for Christian social action is
obvious. Millions of persons are suffering because of war, pollution,
the population explosion, famine, economic injustice, political corruption, inadequate housing, racism, family disorder, crime, drug abuse,
and other social problems. God is not pleased with such conditions.
Christians have a responsibility to strive to lift society toward God's
ideal. By such a struggle they will both help many persons and advance
the cause of Christ.

Evangelism and Missions

Proclaiming the gospel should be a concern for all Christians. Application of the gospel to life is closely linked to evangelism and missions.
Evangelism contributes to social concern and social action contributes
to evangelism. The goal of evangelism is to lead persons to trust and
follow Jesus Christ as Lord and Savior. Such persons, if they understand

the gospel, will care deeply about the total needs of men and society. Thus evangelism contributes to Christian social action.[4]

Christian social action in turn aids evangelism. Christians who act to correct social problems and care for total human need are to do so in Christ's name. Such active concern for others is a type of Christian witness. Christians do not engage in social action solely to win converts, but a Christian acting courageously on behalf of others wins a hearing for his message. Jesus said, "Your light must shine before people, so that they will see the good things you do and give praise to your Father in heaven" (Matt. 5:16, TEV).

Furthermore, application of the gospel to life takes the believer into all areas of society where he communicates with a variety of people such as politicians, labor leaders, school board members, drug abusers, and prisoners. If his faith remains purely personal or strictly church oriented, he might never encounter these people for Christ. Social action widens a Christian's contacts and opportunities to proclaim the gospel.

One of the greatest barriers to world evangelism is the failure of many Christians to apply the gospel to life. The person who professes faith in Christ but fails to follow the teaching and example of Jesus is a serious stumbling block to the unbeliever. For example, mission efforts at home and abroad are hindered by racism in many churches in America. Greed, sexual immorality, hate, dishonesty, family breakdown, and other failures to live up to the standards of Christ undermine evangelism. Consistent Christian living greatly aids evangelistic efforts.

Spiritual Development

Worship and Bible study alone are not adequate for healthy spiritual growth. Christian service coupled with worship and Bible study, however, is an excellent combination for spiritual development. A person encountering and dealing with desperate human need and complex social problems soon discovers the limits of his own ability. He learns that he must tap spiritual resources and claim God's promises to help those who call on him.

---

[4] See Kenneth Scott Latourette, *History of the Expansion of Christianity*, Vol. I, ch. 6; Vol. II, ch. 8; Vol. III, ch. 16; Vol. IV, ch. 5, 10, 11; Vol. VII, ch. 5; and Timothy L. Smith, *Revivalism and Social Reform*.

Institutional Growth

Sustaining the church as an institution is a valid Christian concern. Any institution—including a local church—needs members and money in order to survive. Maintaining the institution is not an end in itself, but the institution can be a means to the end of Christian witness. For example, apart from the institutional expression of the Christian faith, many aspects of the application of the gospel would not be carried out—such as family life conferences, Bible-based teaching against racism, and church-sponsored housing programs for the poor.

Many people will be attracted to a church which demonstrates social concern. Numerous Christians feel that most churches have not done what they should in applying the gospel. Young people in particular often want churches to be active in dealing with social problems, but adults also feel very strongly the need to apply the gospel. A church which relates the gospel in a practical way to current issues will tend to attract and hold such persons.

There may be times when a church or an institution will diminish as a result of its struggle with social injustice. But a church should not set institutional extinction as a goal. Statistical failure is no more acceptable a goal for the church than statistical success. Every effort short of compromise with basic Christian convictions should be exerted to maintain the health and growth of the church.

Social concern in itself cannot be depended on to cause a church to grow. Most people are not attracted to a church primarily because of an emphasis on social action. A program for children, worship, dynamic preaching, stimulating Bible study, and pastoral care are all essential elements of a growing church. Without these the application of the gospel is likely to become mere humanism at best or an abrasive, divisive, destructive emphasis at worst. On the other hand, a church growing rapidly is not what it ought to be if it lacks an emphasis on the application of the gospel in the community and the world.

Conclusion

The bases of the application of the gospel to all of life by Christians and churches are clearly set forth in the Bible. Through the centuries individuals and groups of believers have remained true to the biblical ideal of active concern for total human need without sacrificing other essential elements of the Christian faith. Present needs both within and without the churches call for a continued emphasis on social concern and action by Christians. In light of these facts, each Christian and every church should ask, "In what ways can we apply the gospel to the social issues and moral problems of our day?" The following pages are devoted to helping answer this question.

II
Laying the Foundation
for a Program of Application

There is no one right way to begin and operate a program of Christian social action. Some programs of application are carefully nurtured and developed over a long period of time. Others erupt out of a crisis. Some are largely the result of pastoral leadership. In other cases laymen initiate and carry them out. Whatever works and is consistent with the "way of Christ" can be right. On the other hand, most programs have certain features in common. A general pattern to follow is helpful to most churches—if for no other reason than having something with which to begin.

Here is an approach which may prove helpful to churches in initiating a program of Christian social action:

    (1) Stimulate Concern
        (2) Overcome Resistance
           (3) Establish Guidelines
               (4) Develop Organization

The following pages elaborate on each of these steps. If your church already has a functioning program of application, you may still find the following material helpful. Most of the suggestions relate as much to conducting a program of Christian social action as to beginning one. The next chapter discusses the steps in dealing with specific issues. This chapter, however, is on how to develop a general program of application.

Stimulate Concern

An effective program of application calls for stimulating Christian social concern in as many persons as possible. The task of motivation usually falls to the pastor and staff of a church. Frequently they are aided by laymen who are already deeply committed to the total dimensions of the gospel. In some churches laymen are concerned but the staff members are not. In such a situation the laymen should try to develop the interest of the pastor and staff. Without their approval and support, a program of application in the church stands little chance of success. Stimulating interest in the application of the gospel is a continuing project. When a committee exists that is responsible for a program of application, it should see that Christian social concern is emphasized frequently in the church.

Emphases

These five basic emphases will help develop interest in a program of application:

1. Present the biblical and theological bases for the application of the gospel. This can be done in small groups, with church leaders, in deacons meetings, new member orientation, and through regular programs of teaching and preaching.
2. Help the church to understand that Christian social concern has been part of the program of effective churches throughout Christian history.
3. Set forth the current physical, emotional, and spiritual needs of people and ask, "In light of the Bible's message, what should we do about such needs?"
4. Share how other churches are carrying out programs of Christian social action.
5. Show how people can be reached and challenged through such a program.

Methods

Several channels are available for an emphasis on application. Here are some possible ways to get across the need for social concern:

1. _Preaching_ affords an opportunity to make all five of the basic emphases listed above. Sermons can both inform and inspire. Preaching which effectively motivates church members to Christian social action does not usually major on detailed analysis of and solutions for current problems. Rather it stresses the basic claims of the gospel in both personal and social dimensions. To

preach exclusively on subjects such as open housing, race relations, pollution, and war is presumptuous. No one is qualified to deliver an expert word on all of these problems from week to week. Furthermore, it is self-defeating, for people soon grow weary of a steady diet of any single Christian truth. Sermons on basic subjects such as sin of man and the grace of God, the life and work of Jesus, the demands of God for love and justice, and the challenge of the Christian life, when applied to current needs, are likely to evoke a desired positive response.

2. *The program of Christian education* in a church can be used to stress application. Materials from the Sunday School Board often carry this emphasis. Pamphlets and resource papers from the Christian Life Commission of the Southern Baptist Convention are available for studies in applied Christianity. Woman's Missionary Union and Brotherhood mission action materials are also helpful although they are oriented to ministry rather than application.

3. *Small groups* can engage in special research, prayer, Bible study, reading, and discussions about the need for the application of the gospel.

4. *Retreats* can be planned to introduce various groups in the church—deacons, Sunday School leaders, youth, officers, committee members—to the concepts of Christian social concern and action.

5. *Tours* of the community offer a chance for people to learn about local problems and see the need for dealing with them.

6. *Books, tracts, and other material* on application can stimulate interest. See the chapter on "Resources for Application" for suggested reading material.

7. *Visits from or to other churches* with effective programs of Christian social action enable people to grasp quickly what can be done in such programs.

8. *Mission action* groups and ministry projects sponsored by Brotherhood and WMU organizations can lead to more comprehensive programs of application.

9. *Special conferences or programs* on applied Christianity can in-

crease social concern. Various names are used for these conferences—Christian Life Conference, Christian Life Revival, Bible
and Life Week, Faith and Work Conference. The programs are
designed to present the bases, needs, and opportunities for applied
Christianity. Sometimes a "county fair" theme is carried out with
booths to present various community needs and programs designed to meet those needs. [See pages 133-135 for sample
programs of such conferences.]

10. *Listening teams* may be formed to attend meetings of the school
board, city council, commissioner's court, community action
councils, hospital boards, legislative hearings, ecology action
groups, and other such meetings, and to report to the church
on what they find.

Overcome Resistance

The pastor or whoever presents the idea of a program of application
should make his appeal in a way to gain maximum affirmative response.
Overcome resistance whenever possible. Carefully answering objections
and dealing helpfully with those who oppose the program are effective
ways to decrease negative reaction. It is important to gain a positive
response from as many members of the congregation as possible.

Presenting the Program

The following suggestions will help win support for a program of
application:

1. *Stress the biblical basis for application.* An appeal to apply the
church's message to the community and to the world should be
based on the Bible. Most Baptists respect the authority of the
Bible. They are more likely to back a program which is clearly
biblical than one which is not. The biblical basis for application
should be presented often in sermons, Bible studies, articles, and
discussions.

2. *Be positive.* Stress what can be done and what opportunities are
available. Praise existing efforts on behalf of applied Christianity
in the church and assume that the members want to expand their
Christian outreach. Don't emphasize past failures to apply the

gospel, ridicule present efforts, scold the people for inactivity, or display sarcasm. Such approaches would only stir up resistance. They could lead to rejection of the proposed program.

3. *Maintain a good relationship.* Little can be accomplished without a good relationship between leader and people. People must feel that their leader is a responsible person who can be trusted and who desires their best interests. Integrity and careful planning are essential on his part. In some ways a man who has been pastor of a church for many years and has built up a reservoir of goodwill can move with more dispatch in programs of application than a pastor newly arrived. A pastor usually comes to a church, however, with the goodwill of the people and can begin immediately to lead in new programs.

4. *Stress a connection with tradition as well as the challenge of the new.* Some church members are by nature suspicious of new programs and comfortable with traditional approaches. These people should be helped to understand that programs of application are in keeping with, not a departure from, Christian tradition. Strong churches, small and large, have always been concerned about the application of the gospel. Specific programs and approaches have varied through the centuries, but meeting total need has remained a goal of dedicated Christians.

Other church members like to be part of that which is new and creative. They tend to be critical of the traditional. Such persons should be made aware of fresh, innovative approaches to Christian social action. They should be challenged to be a part of new programs designed to bring about social change that helps people and glorifies God.

5. *Relate application to survival.* Application is more likely to be an asset to growth and vitality than to decline and weakness in a church. In some cases, however, social action may result in a loss of membership. For instance, prejudiced people may part company with a church which determines to open its doors to all people regardless of race. Normally, however, application can contribute significantly to those things necessary for institutional survival—the blessings of God, members, money, facilities. People

are attracted to a church which cares in deed as well as word. Programs of application close to home often stimulate participation and contributions. It is important that a leader communicate to the people that application can contribute to church vitality.

6. *Avoid a one-sided approach.* A church should not build its entire life around social action any more than it should build its entire life around education. Aggressive programs of missions, evangelism, visitation, enlistment, ministry, and stewardship are also necessary. Many people are first attracted to a church for what they can receive, not for what they can contribute. Some of these may be substandard Christians, but many are hurt people needing help. They should be welcomed. Through nurture they can be expected to grow toward maturity in Christ. Worship, fellowship, Christian education, ministry, and witness as well as programs of application are essential in the life of a church if such growth is to take place.

A pastor should avoid putting all of his energy into dealing with social problems outside of the church. People within the church often need help as much as those on the outside. Prophetic preaching on social issues is important, but so also is preaching to comfort and guide individual Christians. People need to be assured that the pastor will not forget them in his zeal to apply the gospel in the community. Without this assurance many will not enthusiastically support a program of Christian social concern and action.

Answering Objections

Some people may sincerely object to a program of application. Their reasons should be carefully considered and dealt with. Here are some of the more common objections with suggested responses:

Theological Objections to Social Action. The following theological arguments against a program of Christian social action may be encountered.

1. *Objection:* "Only God can make a perfect world; we should not presume to do what only God can do."

Reply: True, only God can make a perfect world. According to the Bible, however, Christians are responsible for meeting human need and attempting to correct conditions which harm human life. As we carry out these responsibilities we may contribute to developing better communities and a better world. We are to act out of godly concern for men even though our human limitations rule out perfect success.

Furthermore, inability to achieve perfection does not cause us to give up other activities. There are no perfect churches, sermons, or marriages. Yet Christians continue to establish churches, preach sermons, and get married. If we had to be assured of perfection, we would never do any of these. But we do them because we feel that we should, even though we know we will not do them perfectly. The same should be true with efforts to combat social injustice.

2. *Objection:* "Social concern is liberalism."

Reply: It is tragic for conservatives to avoid social action because liberals may be involved in it. Many social action movements have been led by theological conservatives. The Christian's position must be determined by God's will, not by the stand of others and by what is right, not by labels.

3. *Objection:* "Saving souls is the basic task of the Christian, and social concern detracts from soul winning."

Reply: All that a Christian does should be related to bearing witness so as to help others find life in God through Jesus Christ. Application of the gospel to all of life is part of the Christian's witness. Rather than detracting from evangelism, Christian social action can contribute to it. It may seem logical for a Christian to spend all of his time talking to people about believing and following Jesus. But such an approach is not biblical. Jesus did not spend all of his time preaching and teaching. Neither did the apostles nor the leaders in New Testament churches. In addition to preaching the gospel to unbelievers, they gave attention to how faith in God is to affect daily life. We should follow the biblical example.

4. *Objection:* "Social action is not the task of a church. The churches in the New Testament did not engage in social action. Other institutions exist to deal with social problems. Churches should

stick to their unique role—preaching the gospel. Individual Christians, not churches, are the ones to carry out any social action."

Reply: Although New Testament churches may not have openly attacked certain social evils of their day, such as slavery, they did deal with social problems. The greed, pride, prejudice, and class hatreds of the ancient world were met head-on with the gospel. Crumbling family life was promptly, positively strengthened. Destructive sex practices were openly countered. New Testament writers delivered a far broader message than simply on how to get to heaven. They preached, talked, and wrote about daily work, divorce, family relations, prejudice, sex, citizenship, drunkenness, dishonesty, injustice, and many other social issues. For the New Testament writers, social problems were spiritual problems.

A church, as the people of God, is constantly involved in social action. When members of the church function as responsible citizens, workmen, and families, the church is in social action. One of the most effective ways for Christians to work for social change is through public and private organizations that are basically secular in nature.

More directly, a church as an institution has a responsibility to apply the gospel to life. Preaching and Christian education based on the Bible must take seriously issues such as poverty, citizenship, sex, war, and family life because the Bible takes them seriously. Concern for such issues may result in groups being formed to deal with specific problems. Preaching the gospel and studying the Bible thus calls forth social action. Although such action seldom involves all the members of the church (what program does?), it is nonetheless church related. Christian social action is more than a mere humanitarian or secular effort for social change. It bears witness to the life-transforming power of Christ and his gospel.

5. *Objection:* "Social action by churches violates the principle of the separation of church and state."

Reply: Social action by churches can violate church-state separation. If churches attempt to gain control of government, manipulate the government for personal or corporate gain, or use government money or agencies to spread the gospel, the separation principle is violated. There is no violation, however, if a church attempts to influence government to bring about a general improvement in society, attacks corruption in government, encourages Christians to assume responsible roles in government, enables individual Christians to function effectively as citizens, or shares with the community at large facts or concepts about government not otherwise being presented.

6. *Objection:* "The way to change society is to change individual lives. The best way to change individuals is through evangelism. Therefore, evangelism is the basic approach to social change. All of our efforts should be concentrated solely on evangelism."

Reply: Evangelism is a basic means of changing society. However, social change is a by-product, not a direct goal of evangelism. Evangelism alone does not always produce social change. It will not automatically equip converts to deal with such complex social problems as war and pollution. If changed people are to change the world, they must be aware of social problems and of the technical skills required to deal with them. Furthermore, sin and ignorance—both of which are present in Christians—cause many social problems. Racism and family conflicts, for example, continue to exist even among Christians.

Also, the Bible indicates that Christians need guidance on how to live the Christian life. Becoming a Christian does not provide a person with instant, infallible insight on complex issues, doctrinal or social. Churches have a responsibility to equip Christians to deal with social problems, make ethical decisions, and relate their faith to daily life. It should be noted that the Bible does not deal exclusively with evangelism but is also deeply and persistently concerned with the application of the gospel to all of life. Man is not just a psychological being with spiritual responsibilities. He is also a social being and has social responsibilities.

Other Objections to Social Action. The following practical objections are sometimes raised against a church program of social action.

1. *Objection:* "Programs of Christian social action often cause con-

troversy and should be avoided."

Reply: Controversy is not always bad; it can be constructive and lead to progress. Trouble should not be needlessly stirred up, but some controversy is inevitable. Police action causes conflict. Such conflict could be avoided by allowing criminals to have their way, but no responsible person would advocate such an approach. Entrenched evil must be attacked even if controversy results. Controversy is likely to erupt over any issue which people care deeply about and disagree on. Social action frequently results in controversy. It oftens threatens vested interests or stirs prejudice. For example, efforts to provide decent housing for low-income families may arouse the wrath of slum landlords. Or attempts to open a church or neighborhood to persons of all races may evoke opposition from prejudiced church members. In such cases the lack of spiritual maturity in church members is demonstrated, not the undesirability of programs of application.

2. *Objection:* "Church members do not agree on what is right or what ought to be done about most social issues. Therefore, no action should be taken."

   Reply: Church members are seldom in total agreement on what ought to be done about any issue. Building programs and staff members are often focal points of disagreement. Yet few advocate doing away with church buildings or staffs because people disagree about them. Christian social action is as much an essential part of a church as buildings and staff. Furthermore, church members often disagree on theological issues and doctrinal concerns. Are we to do away with all theological discussions and doctrinal teaching because members can't agree? Of course not. Neither is lack of agreement a valid reason for eliminating a program of Christian social action.

3. *Objection:* "We cannot enlist enough persons to carry out present programs effectively. It would be unwise to add more programs."

   Reply: It is true that many churches experience difficulty in enlisting persons to work in existing church programs. But this difficulty may be a reason for, not against, developing a program of application. Persons whose talents or interests are not being utilized in present programs may find a place in a program of Christian social action. Furthermore, churches engage in programs of teaching, training, music, and recreation, all of which call for large numbers of workers. Since personnel are enlisted for such programs, why should they not also be enlisted for application which has a high and clear biblical priority?

4. *Objection:* "Pastors and church staff members are already over-worked and simply do not have time to lead in a program of application."

   Reply: There is no doubt that such a program will place added responsibility on the pastor and staff. Even though laymen are equipped to carry much of the load, staff involvement will still be required. In light of the high priority given to application in the Bible, the pastor and staff should give it high priority also. Making a place for programs of social action in an already full schedule may require giving up other less important tasks. Involvement in Christian social action so as to be the salt of the earth and the light of the world is not optional. It is required.

Dealing with Obstacles

Persons may oppose a program of application for a variety of reasons. Those who stand in the way of efforts to deal with social issues should be dealt with considerately. Often their misgivings can be overcome and they will then support the program. The following are some of the more common obstacles to overcome in persons' lives if they are to become active in applying the gospel.

1. *Unregenerate church members.* "I don't care what God says." A person can be a member of a church and not be born again. Unsaved church members often will disagree with the outlook of members who are truly in Christ. The only hope for them is repentance and faith in the Lord. Evangelism within a church is often greatly needed.

2. *Lack of spiritual maturity.* "Perhaps God wants me to tackle that task, but I'm just not going to do it." An unwillingness to become involved in Christian social action may stem not from an absence of the new birth but from a lack of spiritual growth and maturity.

Numerous church members have never moved beyond the elementary teachings of the Christian faith (Heb. 6:1-3). Expanded Bible knowledge and enlarged experiences with Christ should help them mature and grasp the urgency of applying the gospel to all of life.

3. *Apathy.* "I'm just not interested." Many people do not aggressively oppose programs of social action. Neither do they support them. They are simply apathetic. They need to be motivated.

4. *Ignorance.* "I don't see any need." "We don't have any problems in our community." "I don't know what to do to help." Every church has its members who are unaware of the problems and issues in their community. They are not interested in Christian social action because they see little to be concerned about. Others realize that needs exist but feel helpless to do anything to meet them. They don't know what to do. Ignorance of problems or of ways to help can be eliminated, at least in part, by providing practical information and suggested remedies for social problems.

5. *Tradition.* "We've never done that before." Quite a few people are reluctant to break with tradition, to try new programs. They need to be assured that Christian social action is a vital part of the Christian faith and heritage. They also should be made aware of how creative and innovative Christians have been in the past.

6. *Fear.* "I'm afraid to get involved." Some people are afraid of social action. They realize that the application of the gospel usually creates conflict and they fear conflict. Others are afraid of bodily harm, loss of friends, or economic setback which may result from involvement in Christian social action. Such fears are often grounded in fact. Being a real Christian can be dangerous. Only the love of God and faith that his way is best can cast out fear.

7. *Prejudice.* "I don't want to get involved with that kind of people." "The poor could help themselves if they only would." Prejudice is a common cause of opposition to programs of social action. Social action frequently is in behalf of the minorities, the poor, the social outcasts. When social concern calls for personal involvement with such people, the resistance can be very strong. The best antidote for prejudice is Christian experience. The God who

is no respecter of persons, the Christ who ministered to and died for all men, and the Spirit who empowers believers without regard for race or class desire to root prejudice out of our lives.

8. *Vested interests.* "I can't afford to deal with that issue." "Sorry, count me out. I've got too much at stake." Persons with vested interests in the status quo are often unwilling to try to change it. For example, owners of slum housing are not likely to support low-cost, nonprofit housing for the poor; horse breeders may not back efforts to eliminate pari-mutuel gambling on horse races; and industrialists who contribute extensively to pollution may not welcome a church campaign for stricter antipollution laws.

Working to gain the involvement of as many persons as possible is worth the effort. Unanimous support is not likely. But many who at first resist can be won. A program of Christian social action—like any other program—needs people to carry it out. Don't assume that only a small group of the congregation will participate. If the program is effectively presented and carried out, many may enthusiastically support it.

Establish Guidelines

Before specific organizational steps are taken, general guidelines for a program of application should be laid down. The guidelines may vary from church to church. They are subject to change as the program develops. The following guidelines, however, will be applicable in most churches.

1. *Distinctly Christian.* A church program of social action should be distinctly Christian, not a mere humanitarian venture. The motivation is the love of God in Christ. The goal is to bring men to wholeness through Christ. Christian social action has a spiritual plus which non-Christian programs do not have. This plus factor should be emphasized, not hidden. It includes Christian compassion, concern for the total person—spiritual and physical. It involves Christian response to the divine imperative to do justice and seek mercy while walking humbly with God.

2. *Biblically Based.* The Bible calls for application of faith to life. This biblical foundation should be recognized. All aspects of human

life are of concern to God. Some matters receive greater emphasis in the Bible, however; and ought to be the areas majored on in the program of application.

3. *Balanced.* Worship, Bible study, evangelism, Christian education, ministry, and application are all necessary if a church is to fulfill its God-given purpose. Keeping all of these in balance is important. Each reinforces the others. To omit any is to weaken the whole.

4. *Flexible.* No church program should be considered fixed and unchangeable. Because both the church and society are constantly changing, a program of Christian social action must also be subject to change. It should be adjusted to meet new needs and altered to make it more effective. New activities should be developed as needs arise.

5. *Comprehensive.* The application of the gospel is to be to all of life, not just certain selected areas. Any issue which affects the welfare of persons should be of concern to Christians. A program of application will cover a wide number of issues if it is true to the Bible. A comprehensive approach covering a variety of issues saves a program from becoming unbalanced. A church may need to work vigorously on a temporary basis for a specific cause, such as a liquor-by-the-drink election. No one issue, however, should consistently consume all the energy and effort. A diverse approach also utilizes the various gifts of a congregation. Too, it attracts persons with different interests. Such a diverse appeal can save a church from being controlled by special-interest groups. It can also save the program of application from being crippled by lopsidedness.

6. *Realistic.* A program should be comprehensive in that no important issue affecting people, made in God's image, is to be ruled out of consideration. But a church should enter only as many specific programs of application as it can realistically expect to carry out effectively. If a church promises more than it can deliver or initiates more than it can complete, the results will be frustration and resentment. Future programs will be very difficult to get underway. It is better to do a few things well than many poorly. Consider successful involvement in a few programs before others are undertaken. A church should strain its resources to do all that it can but refuse to overextend itself, doing nothing well. Since most churches face more issues than can possibly

be dealt with, the determining of priorities is highly important.

Another aspect of realism is understanding how difficult most social problems are to deal with. Vested interests, prejudice, materialism all stand in the way of success. Sin is the cause of social as well as personal problems. And sin is stubborn; it does not easily give up its grip. A Christian, therefore, need not expect easy solutions or total victories. He realizes from the beginning that sin will not be completely conquered in the present world order. Yet he has a responsibility to combat evil.

7. *Preventive as Well as Corrective.* Application of the gospel calls both for correcting social problems and preventing their development. Christians are to care for hurt persons in the community as well as to try to eliminate the cause of their hurt. If a drunk keeps running over people with his car, there are at least five options open to deal with the problem: (1) Do nothing. (2) Take care of the injured, but do nothing about the drunk driver. (3) Stop the car, but do nothing about the injured. (4) Stop the driver and care for the injured. (5) Stop the car, care for the injured, help the drunk, and eliminate the source of drunkenness—alcohol. The fifth alternative is obviously best. A church which has a program for tutoring slow learners is to be congratulated for involvement in this Christian ministry; but it should also consider engaging in programs to do something about substandard housing, malnutrition, inadequate medical care, or racism—all of which seriously damage children.

8. *Unselfish.* Programs of Christian social action by churches should be unselfish. Churches, for example, may try to influence legislation and law enforcement to improve the conditions of prisons, schools, or mental hospitals. They may serve as lobbyists for the poor and powerless. They may protest pollution and war. They may work for the enactment of laws to stop drug abuse. But they should not seek special favors for themselves such as tax money for parking lots, institutions, or worship centers. They should not attempt to use the government to make people worship, join a church, or support religion. A church exists to serve, not to be served.

9. *Humble.* Those active in applying the gospel need a large measure of humility. In their zeal it is easy to forget the fact of human finiteness. They can easily be wrong—if not in their goals, then perhaps in their

methods. For some problems there may be no Christian answer as such, only Christians searching to become answers. For some issues, such as pollution, Christians may have no specific programs. They must sometimes depend on the technical training and skills of others. Christian social action carried on by proud, arrogant men, too sure of themselves and too forgetful of human limitations, can be destructive.

10. *Compassionate.* Christian social concern is in danger of becoming only that—concern about society with little regard for persons. Social activists are in constant danger of caring about social institutions while being insensitive to individual persons. Some seem to love humanity, but really don't care for individuals. The gospel is to be applied to individuals as well as to social institutions. According to Jesus, even one's enemies—those who act unjustly and cruelly—are to be loved. Opponents of Christian social action are not to be brushed aside as mere obstacles to be overcome. They are to be treated with the dignity deserved by all people made in the image of God. The corrupters of society, such as racists, drug pushers, pornographers, dishonest politicians, and greedy businessmen, are to be regarded with compassion. They too are persons for whom Christ died.

11. *Cooperative.* While some programs of Christian social action can be carried out adequately by a single congregation, many require cooperation with others. Other churches, associations of churches, church-related action groups, private and government agencies, interchurch organizations, and citizens' groups are all possibilities for cooperative action.

By observing these basic guidelines, a church can avoid many pitfalls which endanger a program of application. Christian social action is perilous enough at best. It is imperative to avoid as many difficulties as possible. A less controversial program can survive mistakes which will destroy one devoted to the application of the gospel to all of life. These guidelines will help a church steer clear of disaster in social action.

Develop Organization

Everyone's business is no one's business. Some group must bear the basic responsibility for planning and carrying out programs if effective work is to be done. Organization is necessary for all aspects of a church—worship, Christian education, evangelism, missions, ministry, and application. Just as a body needs a skeleton, so Christian social action needs an organized structure in order to function effectively.

The persons enlisted to carry out the program of application are more important than the structure of the organization. Able, concerned people will find a way to get a job done. The most carefully developed organization will fail if the persons involved are incompetent or unconcerned. The ideal, of course, is an organization which enables competent persons to work with the greatest possible effectiveness. A program of application can begin by locating leaders in the church who are already concerned about social issues. Such leaders are ideal to start an emphasis on application. They can exert influence through the organizations of the church, such as the Sunday School, deacons, Brotherhood, and Woman's Missionary Union. They can become the nucleus for social action efforts in the church.

Those responsible for a program of application should be trained. Only with training can they function effectively. This book can be used as the basis for an introductory training course. Various units related to training in application are published in adult and youth Church Training publications of the Baptist Sunday School Board. Brotherhood and WMU mission action materials are also helpful in developing trained leadership in application. Additional help can be secured by attending conferences on application sponsored by the Christian Life Commission of the Southern Baptist Convention, by state Baptist agencies, and by other groups.

While organization for the application of the gospel is essential, exactly what shape the organization should take depends on many factors—the size and location of the church, the nature of the community, the characteristics of the church members, available financing and leadership, and which issues are the most demanding. The organization for application should not be a prepackaged, ready-made import from the Christian Life Commission or another church. Valuable ideas and insights can be gained from others, but a program should be worked out specifically for a specific church.

Programs of application are frequently conducted in churches apart from a formal organization for Christian social action. Individuals, groups of church members acting independently of the church, Sunday School groups, Brotherhood and WMU organizations, and youth groups, for example, sometimes engage in programs of application. Such actions are perfectly appropriate expressions of Christian social concern. This section, however, deals with a formal church-related organization designed specifically to carry out a program of application. Here are two distinct approaches to organization.

A Christian Life Committee

1. Structure

Items to consider in establishing a committee for social action include the name, size, membership, form, and budget.

a. *Name.* The group charged with the basic responsibility of directing a program of application is usually named the Christian Life Committee.

b. *Size.* The size of the committee will depend to a large degree on the size of the church. A minimum of three and a maximum of nine persons are the best outside limits in regard to size. Of course, scores of people may be involved in application who do not officially serve on the committee. The committee which directs the program should not be so small as to be ineffective or so large as to be unwieldy.

c. *Members.* The committee chairman, and possibly the members, should be elected by the church along with the other major church officers and committees. Some churches may find it helpful for organizations of the church to be represented on the committee—the Sunday School, the Training Union, the deacons, and the Brotherhood and WMU organizations. For example, Brotherhood and WMU mission action leaders may serve on this committee. The committee should be composed of representative persons from throughout the church including the young and the old, men and women. Members of the committee should have a clear commitment to applied Christianity. They should be able to handle controversy creatively. It is helpful to have members with professional skills related to application. Lawyers, politicians, social workers, sociologists, and teachers, for example, often can bring their training and skill to bear on social problems.

Spiritual depth, tough-mindedness, and compassion are essential in-gredients for those working in social action. Hostile, cynical people can quickly wreck any program, but are especially subversive in pro-grams of application in a church. Those in social action need a sense of divine purpose, for they will be misunderstood and attacked. They should be calm and disciplined, for they may experience harassment and pressure. A sense of humor is helpful, for they will inevitably confront depressing circumstances. Persistence is vital, for their task is difficult and failure frequent.

The chairman convenes meetings, makes program assignments, and coordinates the work of the committee. One of his chief tasks is to prevent the committee from falling into a routine of meeting just to meet. Reports and paperwork are to be kept to a minimum. Action is the purpose of the committee, not just talk, study, mere existence.

d. *Form.* The internal structure of the committee will vary according to its size. In large churches it may be desirable to have a separate subcommittee to deal with each major area of application, such as family life, citizenship, race, economics and daily work, and special moral concerns. Subcommittees can also be set up according to tasks such as research, education, and direct action (see chapter IV for suggestions on approaches for such subcommittees). Smaller churches may have fewer subcommittees or none at all with the Christian Life Committee itself carrying out projects. In addition to standing commit-tees on the basic areas of concern, special task forces may be needed from time to time to deal with short-term crisis problems, such as a conflict over public funding of parochial schools, school desegregation, or an election called to vote on laws related to alcohol.

Three sample organizational structures appear on the following pages. By putting various features together in different combinations other structures can be developed.

Plan A

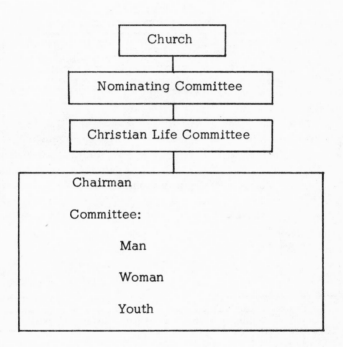

This is the simplest structure, suitable for small churches. The committee as a whole leads out in functions such as Christian Life Conferences, Christian Home Emphases, Get-Out-the-Vote Campaigns; and it assists other organizations, such as the Woman's Missionary Union and Brotherhood, in application.

Plan B

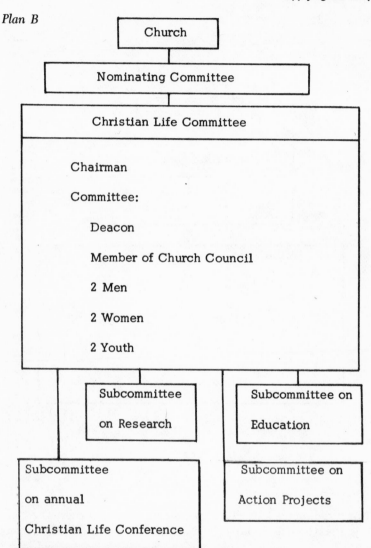

This structure is based on the general functions of the committee—

research, education, and action. The committee determines what emphases need to be made or issues dealt with and divides the necessary work among subcommittees.

Plan C

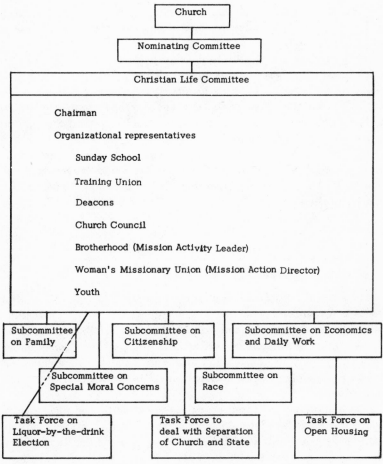

This structure is built around issues. The committee functions with standing subcommittees and temporary task forces. The Christian Life Committee members serve as chairmen of the subcommittees and give guidance to the overall program. Other church members are enlisted to serve on the subcommittees. The members of the committee serve two basic functions: First, they channel the application emphasis to the organizations of the church. For example, the representative from the Sunday School should help plan and promote emphases on application in the Sunday School. Second, they work in a specific area of concern, such as family life, to develop helpful church programs. In this capacity they serve on subcommittees and task forces of the Christian Life Committee. The *subcommittees* are *standing* committees to deal with continuing areas of concern. The *task force* groups are created to deal with *short-term*, often crisis-type, problems; when they are no longer needed, the task forces are disbanded.

e. *Budget.* The budget for the committee should be part of the church budget. The committee should submit a budget request to the church finance or budget committee. Extra funds may be needed for special projects, such as an unexpected election called on alcohol or for an emergency education program on drug abuse. If the money is not available from the church budget, other sources may sometimes be utilized such as individuals or foundations.

2. *Areas of Concern*

The areas of possible concern for the committee are numerous. Most issues come under one of five major categories: family, citizenship, race relations, economics, and daily work, and special moral concerns. These categories sometimes overlap. Housing problems, for example, relate to family life, citizenship, economics, and racial prejudice. A group responsible for one area may need to work closely with one in another area.

The committee has three primary responsibilities in each area of concern—research, education, and action. Research is necessary to gather adequate up-to-date information on issues. Education informs the church and community about the issues, and should be designed to stir concern and lead to more direct action. Action dealing with a social problem can take many forms but some action is necessary if change is to take place. The following chapter will discuss more thoroughly these three functions of the committee.

3. Relation to Others

If it is to function effectively, the Christian Life Committee must relate to the church as a whole, to the denomination, to other churches, and to the community.

a. *Relation to church.*   Normally, the committee's most direct relation to the church staff will be with the pastor. In some churches a staff member other than the pastor, such as the minister of education or associate pastor, may guide the program of application. A church may want to establish a special staff position to coordinate programs of application. Seminaries are now training persons who are especially qualified for this type of work. The committee should work closely with the WMU and Brotherhood organizations in mission action programs. It may also work with the missions committee, church council, youth, and deacons. Each of these can play a significant role in a program of application.

b. *Relation to denomination.*   Certain denominational programs have been established to assist churches in programs of application. (See the "Resources for Application" chapter for a list of agencies carrying out or assisting with programs of application.) These agencies will send you, on request, materials and notices of helpful conferences. When possible, they will help you plan programs and meetings. Many Baptist associations also have Christian Life Committees which can help coordinate and carry out application programs.

c. *Relation to other churches.*   Other Baptist churches and churches of other denominations also have social concerns committees. Some programs can be more effectively carried out in cooperation with other churches. Effective campaigns for improved race relations, better recreational facilities for youth, or stricter enforcement of laws regulating the sale of alcohol, for example, call for cooperation by a number of churches from several denominations.

d. *Relation to community.*   The committee should contact public and private social concerns agencies in the community. Cooperative activities can often be worked out with these groups. For instance, such agencies often need volunteer workers; a church can help supply these. Many churches have unused facilities during the week which a secular social concerns agency could utilize. An agency or individual can supply expert guidance in establishing a specific program of application, such as job training. See pages 72-74 for a list of offices and agencies in a community with which a church might work in a program of application.

Alternate Ways of Organizing

A Christian Life Committee is not the only means of organizing a program of application. Some churches carry out extensive social action projects without such a committee. Each church should find the approach best suited to it. Here are some alternate ways of organizing a program of application.

1. Utilize Existing Organization

The usual organizations in a church, such as the church council, deacons, Sunday School, Training Union, Woman's Missionary Union, Brotherhood, youth groups, and the missions committee can be a vital part of a program of application.

a. *Church Council.* A church council can serve as a clearinghouse for various projects of social concern. It can determine which church organization should take the lead in a project. It can lead the church to establish special committees to handle projects or programs such as alcohol education or a Christian Life Conference. The Church Training director, the Woman's Missionary Union director, or the Brotherhood representative are likely prospects for heading up a social action project.

b. *Deacons.* Some churches are organized in such a way that the deacons function as the primary group in developing church policy. Deacons can lead effectively in a program of application. A deacons' community relations committee, for example, may be designated to function much as a Christian Life Committee functions. Committees headed by deacons, but not composed exclusively of deacons, can investigate community issues and bring recommendations to the church for programs of action. By their individual attitudes and actions the deacons can set a significant example of Christian social concern.

c. *Sunday School.* In many churches the Sunday School is the largest organization of the church. Although not primarily concerned with social action, the Sunday School can play an important role in application. Some Bible study units quite naturally lead to Christian action in response to a social problem. Class projects can center in meeting social needs or solving social problems.

d. *Training Union.* The program of Church Training of the Southern Baptist Convention deals with Christian ethics as one major area of emphasis. Therefore, a number of training programs deal with application. A variety of training resources for social action are available. The Training Union can be used to train persons for specific social concern tasks. Or it can stimulate interest in certain issues and lead to the formation of action groups or task forces.

e. *WMU and Brotherhood.* The various programs for local churches carried out under the guidance of the Woman's Missionary Union and the Brotherhood Commission are related to application. They give attention to Christian social concern, especially through mission action projects. Most of these projects are in the area of social ministry, however, rather than social action. Churches with strong programs for Baptist Women and Baptist Men may consider these organizations as their chief agents for carrying out Christian social action.

f. *Youth Groups.* Numerous churches have active youth programs. Youth can serve in many phases of a program of Christian application. For example, they can carry out educational emphases on drug abuse, unite to clean up pornography in the community, spark get-out-the-vote efforts at elections, and work for racial harmony in schools. A youth council or a committee composed primarily of young people can direct selected social concerns programs.

g. *Church Missions Committee.* The duties of the church missions committee are primarily related to the study of local mission needs and to the meeting of those needs. It may, however, properly assume some responsibility in the area of application. It may lead the church to engage in "action that goes beyond treating symptoms and attack the causes of problems," and it may press for "community action in public affairs."

2. Work Through Special Groups

Programs of application can also be carried out by groups in the church formed for specific purposes. The groups can be either official or unofficial. In some instances the church staff will need to lead in forming special groups for application. They can help these groups by providing guidance and encouragement.

a. *Informal groups.* People from the church may simply gather together to meet a need without seeking any church endorsement of their effort. For example, a group of people concerned about drug abuse may form a committee or task force to sponsor programs of education and rehabilitation.

b. *Official groups.* Other groups may be formed by official church action to deal with specific issues or carry out a particular program. For example, the church might authorize a committee to plan and conduct a Christian Life Conference. Or a committee might be appointed to deal with a specific problem, such as housing for low-income individuals and families. Short-term committees or task forces can be set up to deal with crisis issues, such as tension in a community over school desegregation or an election called to determine the status of gambling in a state.

3. Encourage Individuals

Social action is not always a group activity. There are certain kinds of action an individual can do. The preaching and educational program of the church should encourage individual participation in social action, such as serving on community boards, running for public office, and being a good citizen, family member, and workman. Individuals already in places of influence should be encouraged to use their influence for good. Others with ability and Christian commitment should be encouraged to seek places of influence in order to bring about needed social change. City councils, school boards, and other government positions as well as key posts in labor and management need dedicated Christians with sensitive social consciences.

Summary

Four basic steps are necessary to initiate a program of application.

First, interest and concern must be stimulated among the members of the church. Second, the emphasis should be presented in a way to cause as little resistance as possible, but if objections come up they should be dealt with in a careful, considerate manner. Third, guidelines for a stable, positive program should be established and followed. Fourth, an adequate organization suited to the church must be developed to carry out the program of application. Once a general program has been established, specific issues should be acted on. The following chapter sets forth guidelines for dealing with specific social problems and issues.

Not all programs of application follow this step-by-step development, of course. Some are formed out of the necessity of coping with a particular problem. Then the development is from the specific issue to a general program. Recognizing life does not always follow neat, bookish patterns, the approach recommended in this chapter can help a church develop a program of application.

III
Steps to Specific Social Action

A program of application in a church exists to help solve pressing social problems. It is action oriented. Gaining general church support and forming an organization are only the beginning. Next comes action on specific issues. This chapter sets forth suggestions for such action. Basically seven steps are involved:

(1) Identify Problems
(2) Locate Resources
(3) Evaluate Methods of Social Change
(4) Determine Priorities
(5) Plan for Specific Action
(6) Act
(7) Review and Revise

Identify Problems

A program of application should include plans for specific action. But before action is taken certain steps are necessary. The first is to identify problems and gather information about specific issues. The following are some common problems and issues which may need attention:

FAMILY LIFE

Adultery	Generation gap
Aging	Housing
Dating	Husband-wife relations
Delinquency	Marriage
Discipline in the home	Marriage preparation
Divorce	Mental illness
Family finances	Parent-child relations

Planned parenthood
Relation to relatives
Religion in the home
Sex education

Unwanted pregnancies
Unwed parents
Working wives and mothers

CITIZENSHIP

Church-state relations
Civil disobedience
Communism
Conscientious objection
Cooperation with special
  interest groups
Corruption in government
Courts and judicial reform
Crime and punishment
Extremism
How to have political
  influence
Individual freedoms
Law, order, and justice
Military-industrial complex

Organized crime
Penal reform
Political action
Political education
Public education
Public funding of parochial
  schools
Revolution
Taxation
Totalitarianism
Violence
Voter registration
Voting
War and peace

RACE RELATIONS

Busing
Discrimination in
  employment
Ethnic extremism
Green power (investment
  in minority financial
  institutions)
Inferior health care for
  minorities

Open housing
Prejudice
Racial intermarriage
Racism
Segregation
Separatism
Unitary schools
Voting rights

ECONOMICS AND DAILY WORK

Abuse of credit
Advertising

Child labor
Consumer protection

Cybernetics
Guaranteed income
Inflation
International trade
Job safety
Labor-management
    relations
Leisure
Migrant workers

Poverty
Technology
Underemployment
Unemployment
Vocational choice
Wage scales
Welfare programs
Working conditions

SPECIAL MORAL CONCERNS
Abortion
Adequate medical care
Alcohol
Atomic testing
Drug abuse
Euthanasia
Gambling
Honesty
Hunger
Mass media
Mental health
Organ transplant

Pollution
Population explosion
Pornography
Prostitution
Retardation
Sanitation
Sex abuse
Suicide prevention
Tobacco
Traffic safety
Venereal disease
Women's rights

As needs are identified, they should be recorded. This can be done on a large map of the community, on a chart, or in a file. All of these methods can be helpful. The map and the chart can be used to keep the needs before the people. Here are some ways to discover specific issues and problems in a local area:

1. _Brainstorming sessions_ with church and community leaders. City councilmen, judges, law enforcement officials, leaders of business and labor, social workers, public health officials, welfare agency workers, and other such persons can be very helpful.
2. _Tours_ through your community to observe social conditions.
3. A _fact-finding team_ to explore specific sections of a community and report its findings to the committee or the church.
4. _Interviews_ with staff members of public and private social concerns

organizations, such as those dealing with civil rights, housing, education, or pollution.

5. *Surveys* of community conditions carried out either by a person trained to make surveys, such as a sociologist, or by a competent team of persons from the church.

6. *Guest experts*, such as a professor, a law enforcement officer, or a public official, who share information about issues.

7. *Questionnaires* about possible social problems sent to various people in a community.

8. *Study of census data* to learn about the characteristics of the population regarding such matters as income, housing, and family size.

9. *Findings of church long-range planning committees* are often helpful in identifying social problems. Such a committee, if it does its job thoroughly, will carefully explore and record the makeup and needs of the community.

After issues are identified, gather accurate information about them. Some information will be accumulated while identifying the issues. Here are some possible ways to get additional facts:

1. *Task forces* to concentrate on gathering facts on specific issues. Related government agencies should be contacted. City and county officials can sometimes supply a wealth of information.

2. *Listening teams* to attend key meetings of government, business, and labor.

3. *Conferences* with experts who deal with the issue, such as staff members of local social concerns agencies or professors in seminaries and colleges. A sociology department, for example, will often have extensive information about the area in which the school is located; so also will state and federal agencies.

4. *Books on the issue.* See the books listed in chapter VI, "Resources for Application."

5. *Interviews* with those involved in or hurt by the problem.

6. *Reports and published surveys* on the issue by government, private, or religious organizations. See the list of organizations in the "Resources for Application" chapter for names and addresses of organizations that can help.

7. *Participation* in efforts to deal with a problem is frequently the best way to learn about it.

Locate Resources

After identifying issues, the next step is to locate resources available to help with the issues. Resources fall into four types: organizations, individuals, finances, and facilities. Here are some suggestions about how to locate resources.

Organizations

Denominational social concerns agencies can supply action guides on many problems. See the list of such "Resource Organizations" in chapter VI. Many national, state, and local organizations deal with a specific problem or group of problems, such as alcoholism, pollution, or housing. These government and private agencies can often supply program suggestions. Here is a list of local agencies which are potential resources in programs of application. Not all communities will have each of them. Space is provided at the end to add other agencies, such as those sponsored by religious groups. Fill in the address and telephone number for your area to have available when needed.

Persons or Agency	Name of contact person	Address	Telephone
Alcoholics Anonymous			
Baptist Associational Office			
Child Welfare Department			
Civil Rights Organizations			
Colleges or Universities (Especially the departments of sociology, social work, education, psychology, and environmental studies)			
Council of Churches			

Persons or Agency	Name of contact person	Address	Telephone
Domestic (or Family) Relations Court			
Employment Services			
Public			
Private			
Family Service Association			
Federal Government Programs			
Homes for the Aged			
Hospitals			
Job Training Programs			
Judges			
Juvenile Authority			
Labor Unions			
Lawyers			
League of Women Voters			
Legal Aid Society			
Mental Health Association			
Old-Age Assistance			
Open Housing Commission			
Parent-Teacher Association			

Persons or Agency	Name of contact person	Address	Telephone
Parole and Probation Officers			
Planned Parenthood Association			
Police			
Narcotics Division			
Vice Division			
Juvenile or Youth Division			
Public Housing			
Public Schools			
Public Welfare Department			
Salvation Army			
Temperance Organizations			
United Fund			
Veterans' Administration			
Vocational Rehabilitation			
Y.M.C.A.			
Y.W.C.A.			
Others:			

Individuals

A number of individuals in the church and community are willing and often eager to help deal with certain issues. Some of these persons have been trained in skills useful in coping creatively with social problems. Social workers, sociologists, counselors, teachers, lawyers, and many government workers, for example, usually have such skills. Others with an interest but no expertise can often acquire the needed skills through training programs. Churches should utilize the skills of their members in social action. Persons can be located to help deal with specific issues in the following ways:

1. List persons known to have skills or interests needed to deal with the issue.
2. Make an appeal for volunteers by announcements in church meetings and in the church paper.
3. Survey the church members using a simple form listing key issues. Ask each church member to check those issues he would like to deal with. Request each to state briefly any special training or skills he possesses. From the survey forms prepare a list of persons (with addresses and telephone numbers) for each issue you have decided to deal with. The list should be revised and updated annually.

Facilities

The facilities needed will depend on the type of program being carried out. Some, such as a job training center, will require special equipment and buildings. Others, such as a family counseling service, can be conducted in most church buildings. Many churches recognize that they are not good stewards of their facilities. Buildings and equipment are largely unused except for a few hours a week. A program of application affords an opportunity to use church property extensively. In addition, other facilities in a community can be utilized by a church in its program of social concern. The following are possible facilities for programs of application: church buildings and equipment, homes, schools, mobile homes, apartments, offices, public buildings, vacant buildings, and parks. What is not available free can sometimes be rented, purchased, or leased.

Finances

Most application programs can be financed through the regular church budget. Some activities, however, may need extra support. Here are some possible sources:

1. Individuals within the church or community with a special interest in a particular issue such as drug abuse or pornography.
2. Special offerings taken in church meetings.
3. Private organizations with special concern for an issue.
4. Foundations which make grants for social concern projects. For a list and description of foundations see a book prepared by The Foundation Center: *The Foundation Directory,* edited by Marianna O. Lewis, (New York: Columbia University Press, 1971).
5. Denominational agencies. Some have limited funds available for special purposes. Contact your associational office or Baptist state convention for information.

Evaluate Methods of Social Change [5]

Social change—its validity, goals, and methods—should be carefully considered. Decisions made concerning social change will affect the entire program of application. Faced with a changing society and a maze of social problems, churchmen respond in different ways. Not all agree that churches should be involved in social action. Some believe that churches should not be involved at all in efforts to change society. They offer a variety of reasons for this conviction: "The mission of the church is to preach and teach, not to act on social issues. Other institutions exist to deal with social problems; the church should perform its unique task of caring for spiritual needs. The Bible teaches that regardless of man's efforts the world is going to get worse and worse, not better."

Others believe that churches have a legitimate role in changing society. Churchmen differ, however, about what that role should be. Some contend that the basic role for the churches in social change is to carry out their distinctive functions of evangelism and Christian

---

[5] Much of the material in this section is adapted from an article, "The Role of the Church in Changing Society" by William M. Pinson, Jr., in the *Review and Expositor,* Vol. LXVIII, No. 3 (Summer, 1971), pages 371-381.

nurture. The line of reasoning is this: "The way to change social structures and to correct social problems is to change the people who
comprise society; changed people will change the world. The best way
to change people is to convert them to the way of Jesus Christ and
teach them to follow his way. The role of churches in social change
should be to help God change individuals and to urge these changed
individuals to become involved in changing the world. Individual Christians, not churches as institutions, should be directly involved in social
action."

Other churchmen insist that churches as institutions should be directly
involved in social change. Some of these scorn the place of personal
evangelism and contend that the only way to change individuals is
to alter social structures. Their rationale is this: "Social structures mold
individuals. Conditions such as racism, poverty, and broken homes
prevent persons from becoming what God created them to be. They
can never live as God intended until these crippling conditions are
eliminated. No amount of personal transformation can free a person
from an oppressive environment. Therefore, churches must strive to
correct social injustice and to provide a healthy environment."

A growing number of clergymen and laymen opt for *both* a personal
and a social approach to changing society. They refuse to accept either
a purely "hot gospel" or a purely "social gospel." Instead they advocate
a "whole gospel" approach. They feel that both personal conversion
and social change are important. Therefore, they advocate evangelism
and Christian nurture along with Christian social action. Such an approach is recommended in this book.

Social change may be good or bad. It depends on whether the change
is for a better world or not. But who is to say what is good or bad
for the world? Who is to determine whether change brings improvement? Christians believe that God has set forth in the Bible the basic
standards for society. Our goals for change have been set by God.
Whether change is good or bad depends on whether it advances us
toward God's goals for human life. There are differences of opinion
among Christians about the specific standards in the Bible for the social
order. But there is remarkable agreement on the broad goals. Justice;
lovingkindness; order; adequate food, housing, and clothing; family

stability; peace; an opportunity to earn a living—these are biblical standards for a society. Some would add freedom and security. Anything which hinders human beings from reaching these goals should be changed.

Since a perfect society is not within our grasp, how strictly should we pursue God's goals for society? How much injustice, cruelty, violence, and abject poverty can we tolerate? These are difficult questions. The Bible provides little specific guidance in answering them. We seldom can expect to achieve a perfect standard. Peace, for example, is the ideal. Does that mean all military action is ruled out for a Christian? Some feel it is. Most don't. Apparently living in an imperfect world means we must sometimes settle for less than the ideal as our immediate goal. Nevertheless, the tension remains to struggle, with God's help, toward his ideal. We must never accept proximate achievements as ultimate goals.

What methods should a Christian use in working for an improved social order? Is he justified in using less-than-ideal methods—war, for example—to work for peace? Or lying to get rid of a corrupt government official? The Christian should realize that the means can corrupt the end. He must keep his method of social change in line with the high standards for which he strives.

Methods of Social Action

Numerous methods are employed by churchmen in efforts to bring about change. Which methods of social change a churchman endorses will depend to a large degree on which theory of social change he holds. For example, a person who believes that transformation of individuals is basic will advocate evangelism and Christian education. Those who believe that the democratic process is a key will push for political action. One who believes that change comes only by force will contend for demonstrations, boycotts, and perhaps even revolution.

Here are the most common tactics used by churchmen to bring about social change. Some are more controversial than others. Each Christian must determine which methods he believes God wants him to use. Part of a program of application should be to evaluate the various methods of social change and determine which are appropriate.

Evangelism, prayer, and Bible study are common methods advocated by churchmen to bring about social change. Admittedly few people view these primarily as social action. But social conditions often improve following revivals and people involved in meaningful prayer and Bible study are less likely to create social problems. There is no hope for a significantly improved social order apart from a significant improvement in the character of individuals. Personal transformation is rooted in salvation. Thus, evangelism is related to social change.

Education is used to alter attitudes, stimulate concern, and motivate action. Pronouncements, resolutions, sermons, study groups, books, pamphlets, articles, audio-visuals, billboards, and mass rallies are among the educational techniques employed by churches. National conferences have sometimes been not only an effective technique for education but also a springboard to further action.

Ministry to persons hurt by social problems is a popular means of social action. Teaching the illiterate to read, providing food for the undernourished, tutoring children in substandard schools, developing decent housing for low-income families, job training, and providing capital for black businessmen are examples of such ministries. The intent is to equip individuals so that they can escape from their condition or improve it. While some social-actionists sneeringly refer to this as the "Band-Aid approach," it is a legitimate method.

Setting an example for others is another tactic of social change rather widely employed. For example, many churchmen have worked to desegregate churches and church-related schools, hospitals, and encampments partly to show the world that persons of different races can relate to one another in peace. Some churches pioneer social action programs hoping that other groups will follow their example.

Symbolic protest acts are used not so much to bring an immediate change as to focus public attention on a problem, trouble consciences, or stimulate others to action. During the early days of school desegregation white pastors escorted Negro children through jeering white crowds to protest white racism and to affirm the law.

Martyrdom is a combination of example-setting and symbolic protest. Many church members have suffered obscene calls, threats against family, dismissal from churches, arrest, beatings, and even death for their stand on a controversial social issue.

Mediation between conflicting groups is a tactic employed by some Christians. They have, for example, acted as mediators between land-lords and tenants, owners and strikers, blacks and whites in conflict situations. Their goal is to encourage constructive action rather than destructive violence. In some churches task forces have been set up to act as mediators in community disputes.

Supporting non-church related social action programs. Such support comes in various forms—endorsement, cooperation, personnel, money, and use of facilities. Several church groups and churchmen, including Billy Graham, endorsed the Federal government's war on poverty. Local churches cooperated in government programs such as Headstart. Many clergymen and laymen worked in government programs such as VISTA. Millions of dollars have been channeled from church agencies to civil rights and anti-poverty programs. Churchmen and church agencies have contributed to Americans United for Separation of Church and State in an effort to preserve religious liberty.

Working in institutions with high potential for social change. A number of clergymen and laymen have taken positions in government in order to work for social change. Others have moved into jobs in businesses and labor unions which deal with social problems. Persons in key places can exert great influence for the cause of Christian social action.

Lobbying and political action. Efforts to influence legislation have taken many forms: calls, letters, telegrams to Congressmen; support of and opposition to candidates; voter registration and get-out-the-vote campaigns; marches, parades, and demonstrations in Washington, D.C., and in state capitals; prayer vigils, fasts, public worship services, and preaching on social issues; publication of statements and resolutions on key issues; support of church lobbyists related to state legislatures and to Congress.

Strikes and economic boycotts have been supported by church leaders. Churchmen have supported strikes by migrant farm workers and boy-cotts of businesses involved in unethical practices. On a lesser scale churches have encouraged people to refuse to do business with firms which sell alcoholic beverages or pornographic materials.

Investment of church reserves. Hundreds of millions of dollars are in church reserves. Churchmen are increasingly aware that they have a responsibility to invest this money not only for a return but also for social change. As a result, several church groups are putting their money into banks in minority neighborhoods. Others are using some as "risk capital" for helping the poor and minority members get a start in business. A few are taking their money away from banks and corporations guilty of racism, pollution, or manufacture of harmful products.

Legal action is used both indirectly and directly for social change. Sometimes the churches are indirectly involved. For example, Americans United for Separation of Church and State, an organization involved in legal action to preserve separation of church and state, has been supported for years by a number of clergymen and churchmen. In other instances the involvement of churches is more direct, such as when churchmen challenge in the courts the constitutionality of certain laws. Some churches also furnish legal counsel for persons unable to afford a lawyer.

Marches and massive demonstrations are perhaps the most spectacular methods of social change used by churchmen. The purpose of demonstrations has been to dramatize injustice, to arouse public support for a cause, to influence legislators by a show of numerical strength, and to encourage those hurt by social injustice by showing that someone cares. Television, radio, and newspaper coverage usually gives the demonstrations wide publicity, thereby increasing their impact. Most of the demonstrations are legal. Sometimes, however, especially when permits are withheld, the marches and demonstrations are conducted illegally.

Civil disobedience is a highly controversial method of social action widely used in the past few years. Advocates of civil disobedience have generally followed these basic guidelines: Civil disobedience is a means of protesting an unjust law. Faced with an immoral law, a Christian citizen has a responsibility to refuse to obey that law while recognizing the right of government to punish such disobedience. In an act of civil disobedience a person publicly breaks a law in order to be arrested so that the law can be tested in the courts or public opinion aroused against it. The goal is to get a particular law changed or social practice altered; in this sense, civil disobedience differs from a crime in which a person secretly breaks the law for personal, selfish advantage. Most Christians believe civil disobedience should be non-violent.

Destruction of property, threats, and violence against persons are advocated by a few churchmen who view such methods not as desirable but as necessary under certain extreme situations. Some even approve revolution as a means of social change. Although different persons mean different things by the word "revolution," it is apparent that some are calling for a violent overthrow of existing conditions in order to institute a new kind of social structure. Christians have supported violence as a means of social change. They did in the American Revolution and in the War Between the States, for example. However, the destruction of property and life are extreme tactics with practically no New Testament justification. There are so many other options in our country for social action that churches should not resort to violence.

Each acceptable method of social change can be implemented in a number of ways. People involved in social action should be thoroughly familiar with the various possibilities. This will enable them to select the best approach for a specific task. It is important neither to over react nor under react to an issue. A sledgehammer is not the best tool for cracking a walnut. Nor is it wise to try to use a flyswatter to stop a mad bull.

Determine Priorities

No church will find it possible to meet all the needs in a community. The following questions may prove helpful in determining priorities for projects:

1. Which social problems affect the most people in our community?
2. Which problems are the most seriously damaging to human life?
3. Which needs are being dealt with in the least adequate way by other groups?
4. Which problems are we best equipped to handle in the light of our resources?
5. Which needs do we feel God is leading us to deal with?

The committee should list the problems and issues which seem to answer each question. Those listed most often will likely deserve priority attention. But such decisions cannot be made on the basis of reason alone. Prayer and the leadership of the Holy Spirit should play a prominent part in the decision-making process.

Plan for Specific Action

Having identified the problems and determined which ones should be dealt with first, the next step is to plan for specific action on those with top priority. Priorities, of course, are subject to change. Emergencies may arise. A group of people may develop a sense of emergency about an issue not previously considered very significant. But it is still a good idea to establish priorities and try to stick with them. The group or committee developing a plan to deal with a specific issue will normally gather facts, consider options for action, locate resources, draw up plans, and enlist and train workers.

Get the Facts

Basic to any action program is reliable information. The same procedure can be followed for acquiring in-depth information as is followed in getting a general knowledge about issues. See the discussion on "Identify Problems" at the beginning of this chapter for suggested ways to gather facts about a social problem.

Consider Options for Action

Careful study and research on an issue is, in a sense, one type of action. It is the foundation for other approaches. The committee must determine what options are open and which are best for dealing with an issue. Education, individual action, and direct group action are the most common approaches. In some cases, all these may be needed and in others, only one.

Education. Armed with reliable information a committee can launch a major education program. The committee members can furnish materials for programs, serve as resource persons for meetings conducted by others, or conduct the education program themselves. Information can be beamed at the church, the community, or both. It can deal with the general theme of applied Christianity, with specific issues, or with both. The following channels of education should be considered:

1. *The existing regular educational programs* of the church, such as Sunday School, Church Training, Brotherhood, WMU, and youth groups.
2. *Retreats and church camps.*
3. *Special activities* of the church in the area of applied Christianity such as Christian Life conferences and Family Life conferences. (Contact your Baptist state convention or Southern Baptist Convention Christian Life Commission for assistance in planning these meetings.)
4. *The church library and tract center.* (See pages 128-129 for a list of pamphlets available from the Southern Baptist Christian Life Commission and pages 136-142 for a list of recommended books. State Baptist Christian Life Commissions or their equivalents also have available a number of appropriate pamphlets and tracts.)
5. *The church paper.*
6. *Bulletin inserts.* (The materials from the Christian Life Commission of the Southern Baptist Convention make excellent inserts.)
7. *Displays, posters, and pictures.*
8. *Forums, study groups, and town-meeting style programs.*
9. *Programs for special days* in the year such as Race Relations Sunday, Reformation Sunday, Labor Day, Christian Citizenship Sunday, and Law Day.
10. *Sermons* followed by discussion.
11. *Guest speakers.*
12. *Radio and television programs, newspaper columns, "letters to the editor"* for the local newspaper. (The pamphlets and materials of the Christian Life Commission can be used as the basis for radio talks and newspaper columns.)

Individual action. The committee can strive to motivate and equip individuals to deal with social concerns. It is to be hoped that the educational program will lead to such action. Often, however, individuals must be contacted personally by members of the committee and encouraged to act. Persons should be urged to apply the gospel in several aspects of life.

1. In their normal daily routine in the family, at work, and in the

neighborhood.

2. In citizenship responsibilities—voting, serving on committees, participating in party politics.
3. In existing community action groups dealing constructively with important social issues, such as a human relations commission.
4. By seeking places of responsibility such as elected office and leadership of social concerns groups.
5. By dealing creatively with controversy in the community.

Direct action by groups. The committee may need to become involved in direct action to deal with an issue. Unless the church has officially acted, the committee should make it clear that it does not speak nor act for the church. Churches as a whole do not normally function effectively in direct social action. A small committee or task force of informed, committed persons can usually act more effectively than a church. Sometimes a local church committee can function alone. More often the issue is better handled if the committee joins with other interested persons. A churchmen's committee or citizens' commission can be set up, for example, to deal with alcohol, open housing, or pornography. Such groups may be local, statewide, or nationwide.

Many types of direct action are possible for a committee or group of concerned Christians. (For descriptions and discussions of various approaches, see the previous suggestions on "Evaluate Methods of Social Change." See also the books recommended under "Guidelines for Application," "Programs of Application," and "The Church and Social Change" in Chapter VI.) Here are some examples of direct action: (1) Aid in voter registration of persons from minority groups. (2) File protests with appropriate government officials on racial discrimination in employment. (3) Present a case for workable anti-pollution laws before the city council or state legislature. (4) Work for higher wages for underpaid city workers—policemen, firemen, garbage collectors. (5) Bring pressure to bear on the city council to get adequate city services in the parts of town where the poor and minority groups live.

Locate Resources

Resources for dealing with the issue must be located. The procedure for locating resources in general will also apply to finding resources for dealing with specific issues. (See "Locate Resources" early in this chapter.)

Formulate Plans

After studying the facts, considering options for action, and locating resources, the committee should formulate a plan. The following questions should be considered in developing a plan:

1. What is the nature and cause of the problem?
2. What needs to be done to correct or eliminate the problem?
3. What is our ultimate goal in dealing with this problem?
4. What steps should be taken to reach this goal?
5. How can we utilize the resources in the church and community to deal with this problem?
6. What persons can help us achieve our objective? How do we enlist them? How can we train others so that they will be able to help deal with the problem?

Act

Many groups exhaust themselves in preparation and never act. Talk, study, and preparation become a substitute for application. The committee should not wait to act until they have perfected a plan. Few problems can be adequately understood apart from involvement in dealing with them. A plan can be refined only as it is implemented.

In some cases the committee itself will be able to carry out the program of action. In other instances persons outside the committee will need to be enlisted. It is important when forming task forces or subcommittees to select only responsible, mature persons. Not everyone interested or skilled to deal with an issue should be enlisted. Extremists, emotionally unstable persons, and individuals with bad reputations will likely do the cause more harm than good. (See the discussion on "Members" on pages 57-58 and on "Individuals" on page 75.) Do not overlook retired persons as an excellent source of personnel.

Training persons to carry out programs of social concern can be done in several ways. Here are some potential resources for training:

1. A staff member of the church, such as the pastor or minister of outreach.

2. Persons in the community with special skills, such as social workers, lawyers, college and seminary professors, and staff members of social concerns agencies.
3. Denominational staff members of agencies such as the state Baptist Christian Life Commission or the Christian Life Commission of the Southern Baptist Convention.
4. Classes or courses in colleges or seminaries.
5. Urban training centers and institutes. (Write to the Home Mission Board, Southern Baptist Convention, for an up-to-date list of these centers.)
6. People in your church or in other churches who are already carrying out a program similar to the one you propose.

Much of the best training will come through service. As a person works in a program of application, he will learn about the problem and how to deal with it. This means that people will not be completely trained before they begin to act. They cannot be. Part of training is doing.

Review and Revise

Periodically the plan of action ought to be reviewed to determine what changes should be made to improve its effectiveness. Here are some questions that may help to guide the review:

1. Are we achieving the goal we set out to reach?
2. If not, why aren't we?
3. What unforeseen obstacles or difficulties have come up?
4. How can we overcome them?
5. What mistakes have we made?
6. How can we profit from them?
7. Is the program worth continuing?

Alterations should be made to improve the program. Sometimes the entire plan may need to be abandoned and another developed. Or the committee may feel that it has accomplished what needed to be done and decide to go on to another project. A short-term task force should promptly dissolve itself when the reason for its being no longer exists.

IV
Practical Suggestions
for Application

The following pages set forth specific suggestions for programs of application in five basic areas: Family Life, Daily Work and Economics, Race Relations, Citizenship, and Special Moral Concerns. These suggestions are merely examples of what churches can do to apply the Christian faith to daily life. A compassionate, alert, Christ-centered church can find many other ways to demonstrate concern for all men in all aspects of life. Each of the five basic areas contains several specific suggestions in three subdivisions: Research, Education, and Action.

Family Life

Research for Family Life
Seek answers to the following questions:
1. What resources are available in your community to help families?
2. What is the rate of divorce in your community? Delinquency? Crime?
3. What recreational programs and facilities are available to youth? Are these adequate?
4. Does the welfare system in your state support or undermine family life? How?
5. What provisions are available for children of mothers who work outside the home?
6. Are there organizations such as Big Brothers or Big Sisters that can provide special help for one-parent families?
7. Is there adequate housing for low-income individuals and families?
8. Are all children in your community receiving adequate nutrition, health care, and education?
9. Is adequate prenatal and postnatal medical care and diet available to all who need it?

10. Are birth control information and materials available for all?
11. Are family counseling services available in the community?
12. What provisions are available for the aging in food, housing, transportation, medical care, recreation, and financial support?

Education for Family Life

1. Sponsor family life conferences for the entire community, holding some of the meetings in locations other than the church.
2. Provide group-sharing sessions, conferences, and retreats for those with common interests, such as youth facing marriage, the divorced, the widowed, newlyweds, parents of teenagers, couples whose children are grown, couples facing retirement, and the aged.
3. Keep a tract rack filled with helpful, attractive material on family life. (See chapter VI for a list of the Christian Life Commission's pamphlets in this area. The Family Ministry Section of the Church Administration Department of the Sunday School Board also has materials.)
4. Supply families with materials geared to meet specific needs. For example, when a family has a child who reaches the thirteenth birthday, send them material on parent-teen relations.
5. Ask the pastor to preach sermons on family life.
6. Stock the church library with good books on different phases of family life. (See the list of books recommended for church libraries on pages 136-142.)
7. Arrange for Bible study and discussion groups on family life for various ages.
8. Observe Christian Home Week each year. (Materials are mailed annually to each pastor from the Family Ministry Section of the Church Administration Department of the Baptist Sunday School Board.)
9. Offer sex education programs and premarital counseling.
10. Sponsor a radio program, television program, or newspaper column on advice for successful family living.
11. Stock waiting rooms at bus stations, hospitals, and doctors' offices with attractive, current, helpful material on family life.

12. Take groups of church members through slum areas and lead them in a discussion of what can be done to improve the situation so as to benefit family life.
13. Secure and disseminate facts on government programs for low-income families.

Action for Family Life
1. Provide counseling service for families in stress.
2. Coordinate church meetings to avoid taking families out of the home more often than necessary for church activities.
3. Purchase camping and/or recreational facilities and schedule families to use these facilities.
4. Encourage community and church agencies to offer courses in cooking, sewing, and child care, especially for poor families.
5. Work for improved rent supplement programs and improvement and enforcement of fair housing laws.
6. Form nonprofit private corporations to build or rehabilitate low-cost housing.
7. Work for welfare programs which help to maintain stable family life.
8. Support a planned parenthood clinic.
9. Promote a community child care center for the children of mothers who work outside the home.
10. Lead in forming or supporting a community fair housing committee to work for open housing, improved housing, more housing for low-income families, and strict enforcement of the housing and sanitation codes.
11. Encourage public schools to become community centers, providing such services as after-school recreation for children of working mothers.
12. Work with public and private organizations to make available adequate recreational facilities especially for adults and children from poverty areas.
13. Work to develop public and private programs that insure the needy aging of adequate food, clothing, shelter, and health care.

Daily Work and Economics

Research for Daily Work and Economics
Seek answers to the following questions:
1. What is the average income in your community? How does it compare with other communities?
2. What percentage of the families in your community have incomes below the poverty level?
3. In what ways does your community cooperate with the antipoverty program of the Federal government? State?
4. What job training programs are available in your community?
5. Are unorganized laborers exploited? Is there need for unionization to guarantee the benefits of collective bargaining for these workers?
6. Are some persons paid wages below the minimum standard? How many? Who are they?
7. Are job opportunities equally available to persons of all races? to both men and women?
8. How many persons are functional illiterates in your community?
9. What job placement and employment services are available? How difficult or easy is it to get a job if you are a school dropout, a Negro, an older worker, a young person, a person with a physical or mental handicap, or an ex-prisoner?
10. What is the rate of unemployment in your community? What is it for minority groups? the undereducated?
11. Does child labor exist in the community? If so, under what conditions? Are children exploited? kept from school? employed in situations which are dangerous to their health?
12. Can young people find employment when they want to work during summers or after school?
13. Are women treated justly in regard to employment? Do they receive pay, promotions, and retirement benefits without discrimination due to sex?
14. What is the degree of pollution in your community? Who are the major polluters? What steps can be taken to stop municipal or industrial pollution?

15. Is the economy of your community balanced or dependent on one industry or source of income?
16. Are church employees adequately paid? Are all given fringe benefits including retirement?
17. Is vocational guidance available in your community?
18. Does your chamber of commerce or city council seek to bring in industry with a record of pollution or labor exploitation?
19. How many people in your area are subsisting on substandard diets? suffering malnutrition? utilizing a free school lunch program?
20. Are welfare benefits available for those who need them? Day-care centers for working mothers?
21. What do the public welfare offices and other offices dealing with poverty indicate that churches can do to help improve welfare services?
22. Does the welfare system in your state and community protect the dignity of the recipients? the stability of families?
23. Do people work under conditions which are dangerous or damaging to their health? What is being done to improve such conditions?

Education for Daily Work and Economics

1. Set up a study group in the church to discuss the relation of the Christian faith to daily work, study national economic policies, and investigate the relation of economics to politics.
2. Invite persons who are working in government and private anti-poverty programs to meet with the church and outline ways the members can help.
3. Encourage the pastor to preach on the Christian's economic responsibility.
4. Invite both labor and management leaders to present their views.
5. Stock the tract rack and library with materials on the Christian's responsibility in economics and daily work.
6. Offer vocational guidance to the young people in the church.
7. Teach church members to utilize and/or help in government and private economic aid programs.

8. Suggest that members shop where the businesses implement civil rights laws, employ minority members, and pay a just wage.
9. Invite case workers and administrators of the public welfare program in your area to explain the system to your church.
10. Distribute factual information about the welfare program to dispel myths and rumors.
11. Distribute information suggesting what individuals can do to reduce pollution, such as forming car pools for commuting, collecting cans and bottles for recycling, burying garbage in the yard or flower beds, and using paper products thoroughly before disposing of the paper.
12. Stress the importance of paying just wages and giving a fair day's work.
13. Hold seminars and discussions on subjects such as technology, leisure, cybernation, and pollution.
14. Provide information on Christian stewardship.
15. Discuss in church groups money management, fiscal responsibility, credit, and wise consumerism.
16. Teach concerning the dangers of materialism and greed.

Action for Daily Work and Economics
1. Sponsor a meeting of businessmen in the church to discuss job training, equal opportunities, and ways to decrease unemployment.
2. Operate a job training and placement program or make church facilities available for such a program.
3. Teach literacy classes.
4. Make church facilities available for community poverty programs and urge church members to help in these programs, being careful to observe separation of church and state.
5. Pay all persons working for the church a just wage.
6. Lead in forming a community committee to work for fair employment and wage policies.
7. Find a competent mediator for small labor-management disputes.
8. Place church funds in banks which make loans to minority groups for economic development.

9. Establish a credit union for minority and low-income persons or help a church composed primarily of such persons to establish a credit union.

10. Sponsor group discussions among persons of the same or similar vocation to explore ways to relate faith and work.

11. With care and discretion make emergency relief in food, clothing, payment of rent and utility bills available to persons not covered under public welfare programs.

12. Utilize retired persons and others with leisure time in the church program, especially in ministry and social concerns activity.

13. Investigate and protest when inferior foods and other goods are merchandised to the poor, or when exorbitant prices are charged those least able to pay.

Race Relations

Research for Race Relations

1. What percentage of the population in your area is white? black? Latin American? other?

2. What is the average income for each racial or ethnic group?

3. What is the unemployment rate for each group?

4. What is the infant mortality and life expectancy rate for each group?

5. What percentage of each group lives in substandard housing?

6. Are churches in your community open to persons of all races and ethnic groups? How many actually have a multiracial membership?

7. Is housing open to persons from all racial and ethnic groups? If not, what can be done about it?

8. Are adequate recreational facilities available for persons of all races?

9. Is the proportion of Negroes and other minorities in government jobs representative of the percentage living within your city?

10. Are members of minority groups receiving the legal minimum wage?

11. Are extremist groups operating in your area? If so, which ones? What are they doing?

12. Are minority group children receiving the same quality of education as majority group children? What is the financial allotment
per child in schools with predominantly minority group children
as compared to schools with predominantly majority group children?

Education for Race Relations
1. Distribute the pamphlets and resources on race relations from
the Christian Life Commission of the Southern Baptist Convention as bulletin inserts, in tract racks, and in the church library.
(See page 129.)
2. Prepare bulletin boards on race relations.
3. Place good books on race relations in the church library. (See
chapter VI for the books recommended by the Christian Life
Commission of the Southern Baptist Convention.)
4. Invite members of different races and ethnic groups to speak
to Sunday School and Training Union groups, worship services,
and meetings of the Brotherhood and Woman's Missionary Union
organizations.
5. Encourage the pastor to preach sermons dealing with race relations.
6. Observe Race Relations Sunday the second Sunday in February.
7. Sponsor a conference on race relations with guest speakers, factual
information on race relations in your community, and participants
from different racial groups.
8. Exchange groups such as choirs with churches of different races.
9. Stress that parents should teach their children Christian attitudes
about race and set a good example in race relations.
10. Point out the importance of countering lies about minority groups
and refusing to laugh at derogatory jokes.
11. Encourage church members to join at least one interracial group
and to participate faithfully.
12. Request church members to refuse to join or to resign from groups
or organizations which discriminate because of race.
13. Emphasize the importance of not using racist terms such as
"nigger," "whitey," "Uncle Tom," and "greaser" and the impor-

tance of addressing members of other racial or ethnic groups in the same way you address those of your own group ("Mr. Brown," not "boy" or "Uncle" or "John," for example, with a Negro adult).

14. Urge members of the church to read regularly at least one publication of a minority group.

Action for Race Relations

1. Open your church membership to persons of all races if this is not already the policy.
2. Work for an association of Baptist churches which includes churches of all racial groups.
3. Initiate and/or support a community open housing committee.
4. Establish and/or support a community committee to work for adequate, racially open recreation facilities in your community.
5. Sponsor training programs for the leaders in minority churches to help the poor from minority groups to help themselves.
6. Oppose the establishment of private schools which are racially segregated.
7. Develop a team ministry with a church or churches of other racial groups to work together in evangelism, retreats, leadership training, and social action.
8. Encourage businessmen and labor leaders to refrain from discrimination in daily work.
9. Support legislation designed to fight racial discrimination.
10. Form reconciliation teams to keep communication open between racial groups and to improve relations by working together for justice.
11. See that your church pays all employees, including any minority employees, a fair wage.
12. Ask black ghetto and church leaders for their suggestions on what action you should take.

Citizenship

Research for Citizenship

1. Is the government in your state and community truly repre-

sentative of the people? Who is your state representative? coun-
cilman or commissioner?

2. Do members of minority groups vote, hold office, and serve on boards and committees?

3. Is the tax structure fair and just, or does it favor certain groups over others?

4. Are laws just for all? Are they applied equally to all? Do some laws discriminate against women? members of minority groups? the poor?

5. Is separation of church and state being violated?

6. Are tax funds being used for religious activities, such as nonpublic schools?

7. What is the crime rate in your community? Is it going up or down? Why?

8. Are the police and firemen in your community recruited from all racial groups? Are they well trained? fairly paid?

9. Is there evidence of graft or other corruption among public officials in your community?

10. What are the major problems facing your community, such as transportation, water supply, drug abuse, pollution, gambling, taxation, crime, housing? What is being done to deal with them?

11. Who comprises the power structure or structures in your community?

12. What provisions exist for counseling young men concerned about military service?

13. What detention facilities are available for juvenile offenders? What foster home possibilities? parole services?

14. What are the conditions of correctional institutions?

15. What programs are available for released prisoners?

16. How do the wage scales for public officials compare with those in other communities?

17. Are all sections of your city provided with adequate street lighting? paved streets? pure water? sewage and garbage disposal? police protection? If not, what steps can be taken to move toward improvement?

18. What percent of the eligible voters in your community are

registered? voted in the last election? What can be done to
improve voter participation in the next election?

19. What are the major political issues in your city? in your state?

Education for Citizenship

1. Invite civic leaders and law enforcement officials to speak in
   church meetings on what Christian citizens can do to improve
   government and curtail crime.
2. Encourage the pastor to preach on issues such as Christian citizenship, war and peace, pollution, and religious liberty.
3. Provide opportunity for Baptist young men to help them come
   to a decision as Christians regarding military service.
4. Arrange for church leaders to visit police facilities and ride in
   patrol cars to become better informed on crime problems.
5. Supply the tract rack with material on subjects such as Christian
   citizenship, religious liberty, crime, war and peace.
6. Urge the church library to provide books on subjects related
   to Christian citizenship.
7. Sponsor special studies, forums, and lectures on subjects such
   as "Law, Order, and Justice," "Crime: Its Prevention and Punishment," "The Biblical Teaching Concerning Christian Citizenship," "The Christian and War," "Taxation," "Political Action,"
   "How to Influence Government," "Revolution," "Extremism,"
   "Church-State Relations," and "Communism."
8. Circulate factual information about candidates and invite candidates to address the church on their positions.
9. Urge church members to vote, run for office, serve on various
   government boards and committees, and develop relationships
   with government representatives.
10. Encourage church members to become active in the party of
    their choice.

Action for Citizenship

1. Conduct voter registration and get-out-the-vote campaigns.
2. Direct informed write-to-your-representative campaigns on key
   issues.
3. Develop a program to aid released prisoners in finding employ-

ment and adjusting to society.

4. Support the passage of just tax bills to finance necessary government programs and just wages for public servants. Stand against governmental efforts to raise revenue through gambling taxes or lotteries.
5. Commend legislators, city councilmen, and other government leaders when they act consistent with Christian principles.
6. Help establish needed citizen's groups to work for such matters as clean government, action against organized crime, separation of church and state, strict pollution control laws, and judicial reform to improve justice in the courts.
7. Urge your city government to establish listening posts in the ghetto to hear grievances.
8. Send a person from your committee to attend city council meetings and report developments to the church.
9. Support efforts to secure peace and to move the economy from a war orientation to a peace orientation.
10. Provide legal and/or financial aid to persons who are challenging unjust laws.
11. Organize public protests and peaceful demonstrations when other measures to alter unjust laws or government practices fail.

Special Moral Concerns

Research for Special Moral Concerns

Seek answers to the following questions:

1. What is the extent of alcohol consumption in your community? alcoholism? of accidents in which alcohol is a contributing factor?
2. What is the extent of drug abuse in your area? of accidents and deaths due to drug abuse? of crime attributable to persons on drugs?
3. What is the extent of venereal disease in your community? of pregnancy out of wedlock? of abortions? of prostitution?
4. What is the extent of pornographic material in your community? of obscene movies?
5. What is the extent of illegal gambling in your area? of crime related to gambling?

6. What provision is made in your area for care of alcoholics? drug abusers? unwed mothers? gambling addicts?
7. What provision is made for sex education in your community?
8. What is the ratio of physicians to population in your community? Are the hospital facilities adequate for your area? What provisions are made for medical care for the poor?
9. Are there persons in your area without adequate housing? Are there houses or apartments in your area which are infested with rats or insects?
10. Are equal educational opportunities available for all persons? Are the schools free from harassment by extremists? Are the teachers and other public school personnel adequately paid? trained?

Education for Special Moral Concerns

1. Sponsor television and radio programs to develop an awareness of ethical issues.
2. Stock the tract rack in the church with reliable pamphlets and materials on issues such as gambling, alcohol, medical care, housing, drug abuse, pornography, sex, and smoking.
3. Prepare displays and bulletin boards to present information on these issues.
4. Urge the church library to circulate books and tapes on special moral issues. (The list of books recommended by the Southern Baptist Christian Life Commission in chapter VI.)
5. Encourage the pastor to preach sermons on these issues.
6. Hold retreats, discussions, and special programs on these problems for young people.
7. Ask the public schools to teach courses on such problems as alcohol, drug abuse, gambling, and smoking.
8. Place youth-oriented pamphlets on these issues in places where young people tend to gather.
9. Have meetings with parents to discuss the moral issues in the community and how they affect youth.
10. Present factual information concerning the following in your area: medical care, housing, nutrition, education.

Action for Special Moral Concerns

1. Work for legislation and enforcement of strong laws controlling alcohol, drugs, pornography, and gambling.
2. Form community groups to work forcefully with merchants to get them to refrain from selling pornography.
3. Establish a youth recreation center to provide a wholesome place for young people to gather.
4. Provide a "hot line" for people with an alcohol or drug problem to telephone for help and referral.
5. Help develop community groups to deal with problems such as drug abuse, illegal gambling, and prostitution.
6. Establish task forces to deal with pressing community problems such as malnutrition, substandard housing, substandard education, and inadequate medical care.
7. Form a non-profit corporation to build or rehabilitate low-cost housing.
8. Put into operation needed medical services such as clinics in poverty areas, mobile dental and medical units, well- and sick-baby clinics, drug clinics, and home visits by nurses to teach good health practices.
9. Set up food and clothing distribution centers for persons in need.
10. Monitor morally objectionable advertising, protest to responsible persons, and as a last resort practice selective buying.
11. Tutor slow learners and children from deprived homes.
12. Enlist volunteer workers in the schools to assist teachers in the classroom and on the playground and to work in the library and lunchroom.
13. Set up a scholarship program for capable students who need financial help to continue in school.

V
Examples of Application

The following are examples of churches carrying out programs of application. Although the descriptions do not apply to existing churches, each of the examples is based on a specific church; and all of the examples of application have taken place in some church. Keep in mind that these are primarily descriptions of social action, not of total church programs. Obviously a better-than-average positive picture is presented. Not all churches can experience this much success. Still, the examples show what a program of application can be.

Medium-sized Church in a Small City

This church of approximately 600 members is located in a small city in the eastern part of the United States. The church has a balanced program of teaching, evangelism, ministry, and social action. The pastor is a man in his late thirties with a Master of Divinity degree from a Southern Baptist seminary. Prior to his coming to this church he had been pastor of two similar-sized churches and had been associate pastor in a large downtown church. The pastor is the key to the application program. He has a deep interest in Christian ethics and a firm commitment to proclaim the gospel in all of its dimensions. He is not intimidated by persons who hold strong contrary opinions. His basic personality is such that he is able to deal with controversial issues without being caustic or abnormally abrasive.

The pastor began the program of application by preaching on subjects of ethical interest, by stocking the tract rack with Christian Life Commission pamphlets, and by using Christian Life Commission materials as a basis for a daily radio program. A ministry program by the church also contributed to the program of application. A number of very poor families live in the community. Practically nothing had been done for them. The pastor consulted with ministers from other churches, and together with laymen they developed a program to help the poor. An interchurch committee was established. The Brotherhood and WMU Mission Action leaders assumed primary responsibility for leading the church in this involvement. The families living in poverty are both black and white, and therefore, the program was interracial. A warehouse to store food, clothing, and other supplies was secured. The approach stressed meeting need while maintaining the dignity of the persons involved. As people in the church became involved in the ministry program, they confronted a number of social problems in the community. Realizing the Mission Action programs were geared to ministry and not to social action, the church accepted the church council's recommendation to establish a Christian Life Committee to develop a program of application. A representative cross section of the church was elected to serve on the committee.

Soon an interest developed in better interracial understanding. Materials on race relations were studied in various phases of the church's educational program. The pastor preached on the subject on Race Relations Sunday. Pulpit and choir exchanges were arranged between the church and a Negro congregation. Informal discussions with Negro leaders helped the members of the church understand some of the problems of the Negroes in the community—inadequate housing, unpaved streets, substandard wages, and lack of acceptance and influence in the political scene. Efforts were initiated by the Christian Life Committee to see that the streets in the section of town where most of the Negroes lived were paved and street lights installed.

A statewide issue on gambling also involved the Christian Life Committee. A proposal came that pari-mutuel gambling on horseracing be legalized in the state. The Christian Life Committee established a task force in the community made up of persons from the church, other churches, and from the community at large. The task force gathered information on the gambling issue, ran articles in the papers in the community, purchased time on radio, and distributed fact sheets in the community. They also secured time on civic club programs, in the schools, and in the churches to present the case against gambling. On election day the task force organized a get-out-the-vote campaign which resulted in the community's voting solidly against legalization of pari-mutuel gambling.

The gambling campaign made the Christian Life Committee aware of how little most people in the community know about significant moral issues. The committee met with the public school leaders and asked that courses be offered in the public schools about certain moral issues such as the abuse of drugs, including alcohol and tobacco. The committee gathered materials on these subjects which could be used as resource material for the course in the school. After assuring themselves that the religious issues involved would not be particularly divisive, the school board voted to establish a program of education on moral issues. The courses were prepared, manuals written, resource materials collected, books put in the library, and the program initiated at the beginning of the school year.

The Christian Life Committee decided that a special emphasis on daily work, vocations, and economics was needed. For a start, the committee held a conference on daily work and economics, inviting labor leaders, business leaders, and an economics professor from a nearby college to participate. Interest in the meeting was so great that the church voted to have a series of fellowships in which persons of similar occupations met to discuss how the Christian faith could be related to their vocation. For a period of approximately six months meetings of doctors, farmers, teachers, businessmen, homemakers, students, and others met, studied the Bible, prayed, and dealt with concrete cases on how they could better apply the principles of the Christian gospel to their vocations.

The gambling issue highlighted the need for better information on citizenship responsibility and how the democratic process really works. The pastor preached a series of sermons on Christian citizenship. Tracts on citizenship from the Christian Life Commission were spotlighted in the library. The youth were organized into study groups to find out what particular problems existed in the community and what could be done about them. Books on Christian citizenship were purchased and put in the church library. In the next elections, the church invited local candidates for a Sunday night service in which each one spoke, the people asked questions, and there was an after-church informal fellowship and discussion. The young people helped to organize a get-out-the-vote campaign for the election.

During the discussions of citizenship responsibility the young people became aware that many were confronted with military service without any kind of counsel on what they should do. From the Southern Baptist Christian Life Commission, the pastor secured materials outlining both the options young men can take in regard to military service and the different positions regarding war advocated by various groups. A weekend conference was set up for young men from ages 15 through 20. Materials were given them, discussions were held, Bible study on war and peace conducted, and individual counseling sessions were made available. The monthly meeting of Baptist Men used the materials as an alternate approach for its program.

In addition to other conferences, the church voted to hold an annual family life conference. The Christian Life Committee was assigned the primary responsibility for promoting it. The conference was scheduled for a Friday through Sunday, utilizing visiting speakers. Emphasis was given to the role of the family in molding character and in dealing with social problems. Family needs were found to be so extensive that a subcommittee on family life was set up in the Christian Life Committee to be responsible for a continuing emphasis on family. The church also entered into an arrangement with other churches in the association to provide a fulltime family counselor.

Throughout the development of various programs of application, the pastor has encouraged laymen to take the lead. Through his preaching, suggestions of books, and scheduling of conferences he has attempted to encourage and stimulate lay participation. In the actual projects lay persons have taken the initiative. In the future, the Christian Life Committee is planning to encourage various organizations of the church, such as Acteens, Royal Ambassadors, Baptist Men, Baptist Women, and the Church Training program to be involved in selected programs on the application of the gospel to life.

Large Downtown Church

This large downtown church called a man as pastor who had a deep commitment to the application of the gospel. Before accepting the pastorate he outlined to the people his intention to develop an extensive program of application without forsaking evangelism, education, or other essential programs. The people accepted his proposal. The pastor began with action rather than theory. He appointed small committees to study problems in the city—race relations, poverty, city government, housing, the effects of alcohol and other drugs, and the needs of the aged. The church employed a Christian sociologist to do a professional study of the city and to prepare specific proposals for church programs to meet specific social needs. The church made a survey of its membership to discover interests and talents useful in Christian social action. The information was put on cards and filed so that personnel could be readily found to deal with particular problems.

The church council carried the basic responsibility for the program of application. The pastor and other church leaders appealed to various groups to become involved in Christian social action. The leadership of the Woman's Missionary Union, Brotherhood, Sunday School, Training Union, and deacons were all involved in program planning.

Realizing that interracial tensions generally run higher in the summer than at any other time, the church sponsored a summer recreation program in two sections of the city where ethnic and racial groups were in the majority. These programs were operated primarily by high school and college students under adult supervision. Special mobile recreation units were built for the program. Later the units were used for after-school recreation, retreats, and summer camps.

The church became involved in a number of campaigns concerning moral issues. In a statewide election on gambling and liquor-by-the-drink, the church was a center of activity in opposition to both issues. Utilizing telephone and letter writing, the church members saturated the community with information on the issues at stake in the election. At election time the church operated extensive car pools to get voters to the polls.

The church entered a cooperative relation with other churches to wage war on pornography. Working with the city officials and other government authorities, members of these churches gathered evidence that led to the trial and conviction of pornography dealers. A city-wide crackdown on pornography resulted. Some of the so-called adult movie houses and book stores were forced out of business.

Concern about drug abuse in the community resulted in the establishment of a drug rehabilitation program. Utilizing both professionals and young people in the church, an educational team was formed to share the facts about drugs. A "hot line" was instituted in the church so that persons could call if they were having trouble with drugs and needed immediate help. The "hot line" program was then expanded to include other crises and emergencies. Soon an extensive telephone ministry was in operation with persons from the congregation manning phones around the clock. The telephone ministry now utilizes a complete file, a list of numbers for referral in case of different kinds of emergencies, and a separate phone to fire and police personnel.

The sociologist's study, as well as the studies by several of the committees, pointed up the problems related to poverty in the city. The church was made aware of the need for better housing, reasonable loans, improved medical services, emergency food, and clothing relief for the poor. Calling upon persons in the church who had indicated interest in these areas in the talent search, the church formed task forces to deal with these problems. In two of the low-income housing areas, clinics were established and staffed by volunteers from the church. In one apartment house complex, a small apartment was rented for distributing clothing, food, and small furniture items. A counseling service was also set up in the apartment. The church began to consider ways to help inform the poor about consumer services, finances, and government benefits. Several meetings were held on these subjects, using the talents of lawyers, bankers, businessmen, and government workers.

Finding that the poor had almost no access to loans at reasonable rates, the church, in cooperation with a black church, helped establish a credit union. The persons in the neighborhood were encouraged to save through this credit union. Some were thus able to borrow money at reasonable rates of interest and learned how, in paying back the money, to establish a good credit rating.

The involvement in the problems of the city led to the conclusion that a fulltime minister working with specialized concerns was needed. Consequently the church added a staff member whose primary responsibility was social action in the city. His tasks included many different phases of the city's life and problems. He keeps in contact with various helping agencies in the city, relates to city government, and keeps informed on state and federal programs designed to deal with urban social problems. He assists in securing volunteers from the church for different agencies and groups within the city trying to deal with specific problems. When no group is working on a problem, he organizes task forces to cope with it. He is serving as a catalyst among various racial and ethnic groups in the city to bring about concrete action to meet human need.

The church realizes the importance of a continuing program of education about social issues both within the fellowship and outside of it. Consequently, it has undertaken an extensive mass media effort. A weekly television program and daily radio programs beam to the community the church's concern for specific social and moral problems. The pastor writes a weekly newspaper column on a specific social issue. Conferences and retreats involve different age groups in the church in studies about social problems. The church library and bookstore stock a variety of books dealing with social issues. Christian Life Commission materials are frequently utilized in these conferences.

By maintaining a balanced approach to emphasize fellowship, evangelism, ministry, and education, as well as social concern and action, the church has maintained a healthy spiritual tone. It has also developed good relations with other churches and with the leaders in the city. On the other hand, the church has moved aggressively enough into controversial areas to be the center of conflict. By emphasizing fellowship within the church, the pastor and other leaders have managed to maintain a strong sense of unity without the church's fragmenting into warring camps over various controversial issues. The people have been repeatedly told that they can disagree on the best way of dealing with knotty social issues and still be a part of the fellowship in Christ. The church has grown numerically and financially, setting new records in evangelism and finances. The varied programs of application have strengthened instead of weakened the church, its ministry, its fellowship, and its witness for Jesus Christ.

Suburban Church

This church of approximately 2,000 members is located in an older suburban area which is rapidly becoming a transitional community. The church has an extensive physical plant which includes playgrounds and parking lots. The membership over the past decade had been slowly declining until a pastor was called who had an aggressive spirit concerning all the dimensions of the life and ministry of the church. Believing that the gospel had to be applied to everyday life as well as preached on Sunday, he early declared his intentions to lead the church into an expanding program of application. A group of lay persons, excited about this approach to church life, began to lead in the program.

The pastor guided the deacons in a year's study on the role and nature of the church. He began with a hand-picked number and carried them through an extensive self-study. Then each of them became the leader of a larger group of deacons. Within a year all of the deacons had taken part in a vital depth study about the church. During this time four outside speakers came in to stress the role of the church in the world, its ministry to the total community, and its calling to apply the gospel to all of life. Also, a Christian Life Conference was held, utilizing leadership from the state Baptist Christian Life Commission.

The pastor sought staff members who shared his convictions about applying the gospel. These persons in turn became points of influence in the congregation to encourage involvement of members in meeting various needs. For example, the minister of education developed a series of courses related to the church, its ministry, and its role in dealing with social problems. The minister of youth and music implemented a program of mission involvement with choirs. In conjunction with this, summer recreation was provided in a Negro community with music, art, and remedial reading plus the traditional recreational activities. Discovering that adults were also interested, the program was expanded to include courses in such skills as sewing, cooking, elementary mechanics, and carpentry.

No special committee was instituted to develop this program of application. Instead, the pastor, staff, and concerned lay persons became the focal point utilizing existing organizations and leadership. The deacons and church council became the implementing group for the various projects of application.

During the initial discussion and planning, a number of members left because they did not like the direction the church was taking. On the other hand, other persons began to drive for many miles to come to the church and be part of its life and program. As a result, the church began to gain in membership, attendance, participation, and finances.

One of the steps taken by the church was to decide that persons of all races and ethnic groups would be welcomed as worshipers and members. Few Negroes or ethnic families lived near the church, however; and there was little direct involvement with persons of other races or ethnic groupings. The church decided to team with a black church in the city for certain programs. The two pastors and the lay leaders of the churches met, determined to cooperate in selected activities, and worked out an exchange program of preachers, choirs, and educational leadership. The churches also agreed to tackle a few selected community problems with interracial task forces. One task force was formed on housing and another on employment opportunities. Interracial meetings and cooperation served as an excellent means of educating both congregations about the problems, anxieties, needs, and hopes of the other.

The interracial efforts led the congregation to see that special attention should be given to housing for low-income families, capital for racial and ethnic minority businesses, and job training. Consequently, the church initiated an effort to rehabilitate low-cost housing. It became apparent that such an effort was entirely inadequate for the vast needs of the area. Task forces were developed to provide more extensive programs. One task force established an independent corporation to finance and build housing for low-income families. Another task force developed a community housing council to work with government agencies in developing government-backed housing. The council also encouraged open housing. It struggled with problems in existing government housing complexes caused by inadequate management, lack of recreation and day care facilities, and poor attitudes about the property among the tenants.

The church put its reserves into a bank located in an area of the city dominated by minority groups. The bank is owned and operated by blacks. In addition, a committee from the church has tried to get other churches and church-related agencies to do likewise in order to provide increased capital for racial and ethnic minorities to set up businesses.

Believing that the best way to break the poverty cycle was both to train persons for jobs and to secure jobs for those trained, the church initiated job training and placement programs. The church realized that it did not have adequate information on its own membership to know who was qualified and willing to help in such programs of training. Therefore, an intensive survey of the church membership was initiated to determine talents, vocational qualifications, social concerns interest, and other related facts. The data gathered was put into a card catalog system. Similar information is now requested from each person who joins the church. Armed with this information from the congregation, interest groups were established for job training. Persons in the community with businesses were asked to contribute their facilities for job training in off hours. Training programs were set up for secretaries, mechanics, machinists, janitors, gardeners and nurserymen, and day care workers. People were trained, and then an effort was made to place them in jobs. It became apparent that it was important to have a job for a trainee. This provided an incentive to complete training and avoided a frustrating waiting period.

A number of persons became convinced that the church needed to be more involved in the political life of the city. Tension developed because a substantial number of the congregation felt the church should not do this. The church leadership decided not to involve the church in any kind of partisan politics, to avoid endorsing specific candidates, and to refrain from any attempt to influence the decisions of political parties. The leadership agreed to encourage individuals to become active in politics, to run for office, and to be involved in the decision-making processes of the political party of their choice. The church elected a member of the congregation to be the church's observer at city council sessions and other significant meetings of city government. The observer

was charged with the responsibility of listening, asking questions, and
passing on information to persons who might act on specific issues.
The church instituted a series of "town hall discussions" on Sunday
nights. The format was to take an issue (such as pollution of the river
because of the city's dumping of raw sewage in it), have informed
persons speak on it, and then have a discussion concerning what Christians could do about it. In this way the church informed its membership
on critical social issues.

Feeling that family life was basic to stability in all other areas, the
church instituted a program of family life education and counseling.
A full-time staff member was employed to head up this program.
Utilizing rooms in the church which were used as classrooms on Sunday,
the staff member enlisted counselors, vocational guidance persons, and
psychiatrists to come to the church at certain times during the week
and donate their services for conferences with persons in need of
counseling guidance. Family life education programs were instituted.
The library and tract racks were well supplied with attractive materials
on family life. A sex education series, repeated each year, is offered
not only for youth but also for adults.

Other moral issues are dealt with throughout the year in special
programs, sermons, conferences, and retreats. During the summer, each
of the camps sponsored by the church has a strong emphasis on applied
Christianity. Topics such as family life, race relations, daily work,
citizenship and other subjects such as alcohol, drugs, tobacco, and
gambling are discussed.

The church has maintained a strong program of Bible study with
an emphasis upon prayer and personal devotion. The conviction has
been that apart from adequate spiritual preparation, social action becomes mere humanitarianism. The church has continued to grow in
numbers and finances. It has also developed an ability to deal with
controversy and handle crises constructively. In recent turmoil over
school busing, church members acted as key agents of reconciliation
in the community.

Church in a Small Town

This church of approximately 500 members is located in a town with a population of approximately fifteen hundred people. The pastor, a college graduate with two years of seminary training, has recently developed an awareness of the social imperatives of the gospel. He is concerned about developing a program of application without neglecting the church's emphases upon evangelism, education, and personal ministry.

Since the concept of application was relatively new to the people in this church and the resistance to it fairly strong, the pastor decided to major on education. He began a series of Sunday night sermons on social issues such as family life, daily work, race relations, citizenship, church-state separation, alcohol, sex, drug abuse, and pornography. In conjunction with these sermons he ordered materials from the Christian Life Commission and used these materials as bulletin inserts.

The church librarian gathered materials on ethical issues and promoted their use. The list of suggested library books from the Christian Life Commission was ordered, and many of the books not already on hand were secured. Selected organizations were written to secure materials for the vertical file. Each week certain of these books and materials were highlighted in a display in the library. Also, the pastor made reference to the books in sermons and suggested that people check them out of the library and read them. Leaders in Sunday School, Training Union, and other church organizations were encouraged to use these materials in their work.

Utilizing material in the library, study groups were formed to deal with the application of the gospel in daily life. The groups met on a regular basis on Sunday nights. At first the studies were mainly on the Christian life in general. Then the groups discussed specific topics such as drugs, pollution, sex education, and race relations.

A committee was appointed to seek permission from dentists and doctors to place materials on current issues in waiting rooms. The committee placed material and replenished the supply each month.

The study groups, sermons, and general emphases of the church led to an awareness that certain social problems in the community needed to be dealt with. Most of the young people left to attend college, to work in a nearby large city, or to enter the military. Several study programs for young people were inaugurated. One explored the challenges and opportunity of college. Another helped them understand the city's opportunities and temptations. A third presented options in relation to military service and a Bible study on war and peace.

Although racial tension was not great, the integration of the school system did lead to some conflict. The church was prepared to take positive action because a large number of the people had already been involved in discussions on race and dealing with conflict. Members of the church worked in PTA and in other school-related programs to build a Christian attitude toward race relations and integration. Some members of the church's women's group volunteered to work in the schools as teachers' aides for playground duty, library assistance, and other non-professional chores. This enabled the teachers to give more time to specific classroom responsibilities and to develop special programs for students who came from grossly inadequate schools. Aware of the special needs of some students, the women asked the church to establish a tutorial program. The church inaugurated the program and invited persons of all races to the church after school for study and tutorial help.

The pastor asked the church to schedule a family life conference. The conference, held in the spring, was extremely well-received. It became apparent that once a year was not often enough for an emphasis on Christian family life. Therefore, additional retreats and conferences were worked out during the year. The young people had a retreat that dealt with preparing for marriage. Parents of younger children instituted a monthly after-church get-together to discuss how they could be better parents. Parents of teenagers also began to meet once a month after church while the young people were in a fellowship period; the parents discussed common problems and how to cope with them as Christian mothers and fathers. A large percentage of the membership was over 65, and conferences were held on retirement, aging, and related concerns. A section of the church building was set aside for use by senior adults; provisions were made for recreation and service opportunities. Some older adults served in the tutorial program and others worked in the after-school recreation program for younger children. They found that by helping to meet educational needs and to decrease racial tension they experienced extra meaning in life.

Contact with young people from poverty families, many living in the country, led several church members to realize that many suffered from substandard housing and diets. Also, many poor people had no transportation to get to medical services or church activities. Furthermore, in the winter many had inadequate heat in their homes. A group from the church formed a task force to deal with these problems. Finding other members of the community interested, they established a committee in which some specialized in food, some in housing, and some in transportation.

Gradually this church in a small town has taken on a different character. From being a sleepy institution in which people gathered together one day a week to sing, pray, and listen to preaching, it has become a center of significant activity throughout the community. Increasingly people feel a responsibility to apply the gospel to all of life. Some are dissatisfied with the new direction, however; and since there is no other comparable church in the community, they have either quit coming or have stayed to complain. All in all the result has been positive, however, and the church has moved toward meaningful experiences in application of the gospel.

Open Country Church

This church of approximately 100 members is located in the open country. Most of the persons living in the area are older. There are only a few young families. Farming and jobs in a nearby town are the chief sources of income. The leadership of the church reads the literature distributed by Southern Baptist Convention agencies. Articles in *Home Missions* magazine and in the materials of the Brotherhood and Woman's Missionary Union have stimulated discussion on social issues. At first some of the members were disturbed by the attention given to social problems. But the biblical approach taken in the materials led them gradually to accept social concern as a legitimate aspect of the Christian life or at least not to be as upset about it as they once were.

The church did little in the realm of application. The pastor seldom preached on significant social issues and proposed no programs to deal with them. When he resigned due to ill health, the pulpit committee determined to find a pastor who would lead the church in a balanced program. A seminary student was called as pastor with the understanding he would help develop such a balance. The Brotherhood and WMU, which had practically died, were revived by assuming responsibility for mission action. A church council was formed to coordinate the programs of the church and to initiate action on social issues. The members were asked to submit suggestions about problems they felt the church should deal with.

Several suggested that something be done about the poor condition of the county roads and bridges. A committee of two deacons, two women, and a young person was appointed to investigate the problem. They met with the county authorities and asked for improvements to make the road safer. A polite hearing was followed by no action. The committee then circulated a petition in the community calling for improvements. The long list of persons who signed the petition prodded the officials to act. But clearly some in office were either corrupt or inept. A meeting of residents in the area was spearheaded by the church committee. The people discussed what action should be taken. It was agreed to back a responsible candidate against the undesirable incumbent in the coming election.

In preparation for the national elections, the church sponsored a conference on citizenship. The platforms of the Democratic and Republican parties were studied, representatives from each party spoke, key issues were discussed, and the candidates were evaluated. The conference was held on four successive Sunday nights and people from surrounding communities were invited.

The citizenship conference stimulated such widespread interest that the church council decided to have a general Christian life conference. Sample programs and materials were ordered from the Christian Life Commission and a weekend conference was scheduled. Sessions on family, race, daily work and economics, and special moral concerns were held. Following the conference the church council decided that a program of application needed more attention than it could give. Therefore, a Christian Life Committee was established.

The Christian Life Committee was composed of the same persons who served on the committee to deal with the county roads. The young person on the committee felt improvement should be made in the living conditions and pay of the migrant laborers who worked in the area during certain seasons. Two of the adults felt this was too controversial a subject to tackle. The others insisted that at least the situation should be investigated. The committee agreed to gather facts. Several farmers, when they heard about the committee's action, tried to stop the investigation.

The committee continued its work, however, and found most living quarters to be unfit for human habitation. No provision was made for child care, and most mothers worked in the fields. Wages, while low, were about the same as those paid such workers elsewhere, and by working fast a person could earn a decent per-hour income. No fringe benefits, such as retirement, were provided, however. Armed with the facts, the committee began to call on farmers and ask them to improve the living quarters and working conditions of the migrants. One man, a professed Christian, became so angry he ordered the committee out of his house. Afterwards, in considering his attitude, he began to wonder if he were really a Christian. He had demonstrated no Christ like concern. In a visit with his pastor he made a profession of faith. Immediately he improved the migrants' quarters and meals and made plans for child care. He joined the committee in calling on other farmers, especially to discuss an increase in wages.

The committee, following suggestions from church members, began to plan another Christian life conference, this time on aging and retirement. Also, four Sunday evening programs were scheduled on farming and ecology. The pastor and the Christian Life Committee now have plans not only to maintain this emphasis on application in their church but also to share their experiences with other churches in their association.

VI
Resources for Application

The following provide helpful resources for programs of application. They are from many different points of view. No one will agree with all they say. Yet all supply useful insights. The resources are listed in these categories: Books, Periodicals, Organizations, Additional Resource Agencies, and Christian Life Commission Materials.

Resource Books

Bases for Application

The following books present biblical, theological, and historical bases for application of the gospel. Some are listed which are not currently in print but which may be available from libraries.

Barnette, Henlee H., *Introducing Christian Ethics* (Nashville: Broadman Press, 1961). A Baptist professor of Christian ethics presents a basic introduction to the application of the gospel in the world. Dated but still helpful.

Clouse, Robert G.; Linder, Robert D.; and Pierard, Richard V., eds. *The Cross and the Flag.* (Carol Stream, Illinois: Creation House, 1972). A collection of articles on various social issues from an evangelical perspective. A strong case is made for application.

Collins, Gary R., ed., *Our Society in Turmoil.* (Carol Stream, Illinois: Creation House, 1970). A collection of essays by conservative Christian scholars on social issues providing insight into the why of Christian involvement.

Gardner, E. Clinton, *The Church as a Prophetic Community.* (Philadelphia: Westminster Press, 1967). An analysis of the present social situation, a history of the church's prophetic involvement, a study of related biblical material, and a call for churches to present the claim of God to all of society.

Linder, Robert D., and Pierard, Richard V., *Politics: A Case for Christian Action.* (Downers Grove, Illinois: Intervarsity Press, 1973). A case for social action from an evangelical point of view. Helpful historical material.

Maston, T. B., *Biblical Ethics.* (Waco, Texas: Word Books, 1966). From Genesis to Revelation the author sets forth the ethical message of the Bible showing how God wills for faith to be related to life.

Moberg, David O., *Inasmuch: Christian Social Responsibility in the Twentieth Century.* (Grand Rapids: Eerdmans Publishing Co., 1965). A basic book for both ministry and application. Begins with theological statement and moves to practical suggestions for local church action. Excellent source.

————, *The Great Reversal.* (Philadelphia: J. B. Lippincott Co., 1972). A Christian sociologist analyzes the turn away from Christian social action by conservatives and the hope for future involvement.

Rahtjen, Bruce D., *Scripture and Social Action.* (Nashville: Abingdon Press, 1966). A brief discussion of the biblical basis for social action. Deals more with themes than with particular approaches.

Rutenber, Culbert G., *The Reconciling Gospel.* (Nashville: Broadman Press, 1960). An excellent statement by a Baptist theologian and activist concerning the relationship between evangelism and ethics.

Scharlemann, Martin H., *The Church's Social Responsibilities.* (St. Louis: Concordia Publishing House, 1974). Sets forth why the churches should apply the gospel, how, and in what areas.

Guidelines for Application

These present both general approaches and specific programs of application and social action in local churches.

Hessell, Dieter T., *Reconciliation and Conflict.* (Philadelphia: Westminster Press, 1969). Analysis of church controversy caused by social action. Contains some guidelines for social action. Presbyterian point of view.

————, *A Social Action Primer.* (Philadelphia: Westminster Press, 1972). Sets forth several approaches to social action by churches and church-related groups.

Rasmussen, Albert T., *Christian Social Ethics: Exerting Christian Influ-*

ence. (Englewood Cliffs, N. J.: Prentice-Hall, 1956). Analysis of problems and suggestions of approaches to deal with them. More general
than specific.

Seifert, Harvey, *The Church in Community Action.* (New York: Abing-
don-Cokesbury Press, 1952). A basic work. Although somewhat dated
it is still helpful on basic guidelines.

Wilmore, Gayraud S., *The Secular Relevance of the Church.* (Philadelphia: Westminster Press, 1962). Presents the need for social action
by Christians. Chapter four outlines an approach by a local congregation to social action.

Case Studies of Local Congregations

Fanning, Buckner, *Christ in Your Shoes.* (Nashville: Broadman Press,
1970). Contains a description of some of the programs of Trinity
Baptist Church, San Antonio, Texas, in ministry and application.

Gilmore, Herbert R., *They Chose to Live.* (Grand Rapids: Eerdmans
Publishing Co., 1972). A pastor's account of a church crisis directly
related to race.

Goodman, Grace Ann, *Rocking the Ark.* (New York: Presbyterian Distribution Service, 1969). Nine case studies of congregations of from
100 to 3,000 members in rural, downtown, and suburban locations.
Discusses how conflict in each situation was handled.

Halvorson, Lawrence, *The Church in a Diverse Society.* (Minneapolis:
Augsburg Publishing House, 1964). Case studies on the work of
churches with minority groups and other segments of American
society.

Knight, Walker L., *Struggle for Integrity.* (Waco, Texas: Word Books,
1969). The story of a community church in its effort to minister
in a changing community.

Raines, Robert A., *The Secular Congregation.* (New York: Harper and
Row, 1968). Sets forth the approach to involvement of the First
Methodist Church of Germantown, Pennsylvania.

Shipley, David O., *Neither Black nor White.* (Waco, Texas: Word Books,
1971). A black minister's description of his work in a white congregation. He is pastor of St. Mark's Church, an ecumenical parish, in
Kansas City, Missouri.

Programs of Application

The following describe several specific programs of application.

Greenwood, Alma, *How Churches Fight Poverty: 60 Successful Local Projects.* (New York: Friendship Press, 1967.) A series of case studies of ministry projects and anti-poverty programs.

Mission Action Group Guide: Combating Moral Problems. (Memphis: Southern Baptist Convention, Brotherhood Commission, 1968). Practical suggestions on dealing with issues such as alcoholism and drug abuse, pornography and obscenity, racism, family stress, gambling, and politics.

Schaller, Lyle E., *The Church's War on Poverty.* (Nashville: Abingdon Press, 1966). Examples of ways churches have aided in the war on poverty.

————, *Community Organization: Conflict and Reconciliation.* (Nashville: Abingdon Press, 1966). Discusses the need for organizing the powerless in communities so that they can participate in the democratic process and what the role of churches in such organization efforts ought to be.

The Church and Social Change

Application of the gospel calls for change in society. The following works discuss social change, some from the point of view of Christians and the church.

Borg, Marcus, *Conflict and Social Change.* (Minneapolis: Augsburg Publishing House, 1971). A brief, well-written book on social change and conflict.

Buckhout, Robert, et al, *Toward Social Change.* (New York: Harper and Row, 1971). A textbook on social change. Gives various theories and approaches.

Clinebell, Howard J., and Seifert, Harvey, *Personal Growth and Social Change.* (Philadelphia: Westminster Press, 1969). A blending of pastoral care and Christian ethics. Shows relation of personality, social change, and religion.

Cox, Harvey, ed., *The Church Amid Revolution.* (New York: Association Press, 1967). A collection of papers by churchmen from various parts of the world dealing with the role of the church in social change.

Etzioni, Eva, and Amitai, eds., *Social Change: Sources, Patterns, and Consequences.* (New York: Basic Books, Inc., 1964). A collection of writings showing the basic theories of social change.

Furness, Charles Y., *The Christian and Social Action.* (Old Tappan, New Jersey: Fleming H. Revell Co., 1972). Presents the bases for Christian involvement in social action and deals with Christian social action past, present, and future.

Lutheran Church in America, Task Group for Long Range Planning, *Social Change: An Assessment of Current Trends.* (Philadelphia: Fortress Press, 1968). The results of a two-year study. Evaluates approach to social change and suggests responses by the churches.

Schuller, David S., *Power Structure and the Church.* (St. Louis: Concordia Publishing House, 1969). A realistic presentation of power structures and decision-making and suggestions for church response.

Seifert, Harvey, *Power Where the Action Is.* (Philadelphia: Westminster Press, 1968). An experienced writer on churches in community action sets forth positive suggestions for dealing with the power structure of society.

Conflict and Controversy

When churches move into application, conflict and controversy often develop. Conflict occurs between members of the church and between the church and community. The following describe the nature of conflict and how it can be made to work for good.

Borg, Marcus, *Conflict and Social Change.* (Minneapolis: Augsburg Publishing House, 1971). Presents a study of conflict as it relates to social change from a Christian point of view. Deals with case studies, history, theology, and the future.

Glock, Charles Y.; Ringer, Benjamin B.; and Babbie, Earl R., *To Comfort and to Challenge: A Dilemma of the Contemporary Church.* (Berkeley, California: University of California Press, 1967). Sociological study of tensions in churches over social action efforts.

Hadden, Jeffrey K., *The Gathering Storm in the Churches.* (Garden City, New York: Doubleday & Co., 1969). Discusses basic conflict developing between clergy and laity over theology, social action, and civil rights. Shows correlation between theological and social beliefs and influence of age, denomination, and theology on political and economic belief.

Hessel, Dieter T., *Reconciliation and Conflict*. (Philadelphia: Westminster Press, 1969). An analysis of controversy in the churches over social action and suggestions on what to do about it. Basically sympathetic with social action by churches.

Lee, Robert, and Galloway, Russel, *The Schizophrenic Church: Conflict over Community Organization*. (Philadelphia: Westminster Press, 1969). Shows conflict of two views in churches: those who are social activists and want to become actively involved in social change and those who see the role of the church as more priestly and comforting. Helpful to see what conflicts to expect as ministry moves into application.

Resource Periodicals

Christian Century. A nondenominational journal. Editorials and articles on matters of religious, political, and social concern. Book reviews and news of the Christian world.

Christian Century Foundation, 407 S. Dearborn Street, Chicago, Illinois 60605.

Christian Faith in Action. A mimeographed newsletter published by the Christian Life Commission of the Baptist General Convention of Texas. Carries news items, quotes, and statistics related to current issues. Sent upon request.

208 Baptist Building, Dallas, Texas 75201.

Christianity and Crisis. Published by Christianity and Crisis, Inc. An intellectual Protestant publication devoted to the role of the Christian in today's world. Articles by ministers, educators, scientists, and statesmen.

537 W. 121st Street, New York, N. Y. 10027.

Christianity Today. Articles, editorials, and news features discuss contemporary events of interest to religious leaders in relation to the underlying theological issues. For clergymen and laymen.

1012 Washington Building, Washington, D. C. 20005.

Engage/Social Action. Published by the Board of Church and Society of the United Methodist Church in cooperation with the Center for

Social Action of the United Church of Christ. Materials on current
social issues from a church-related and general point of view.
100 Maryland Avenue, N.E., Washington, D. C. 20002.

Home Missions. Publication of Home Mission Board of the Southern
Baptist Convention.
1350 Spring Street, N.W., Atlanta, Georgia 30309.

Royal Service. Published by Woman's Missionary Union, affiliated with
the Southern Baptist Convention.
600 North 20th Street, Birmingham, Alabama 35203.

Saturday Review of the Society. Deals in a non-religious way with the
issues affecting society today.
Saturday Review, Inc., 380 Madison Avenue, New York, N. Y. 10017.

World Mission Journal. Published by the Brotherhood Commission of
the Southern Baptist Convention.
1548 Poplar Avenue, Memphis, Tennessee 38104.

Resource Organizations

Southern Baptist Convention Agencies

Brotherhood Commission, 1548 Poplar Avenue, Memphis, Tennessee
38104

Christian Life Commission, 460 James Robertson Parkway, Nashville,
Tennessee 37219.

Home Mission Board, 1350 Spring Street, N.W., Atlanta, Georgia
30309.

Sunday School Board, 127 Ninth Avenue, N., Nashville, Tennessee
37234.

Woman's Missionary Union, 600 N. 20th Street, Birmingham, Alabama 35203.

Other Southern Baptist Related Resource Organizations

Many Baptist state conventions related to the Southern Baptist Convention have departments which deal with application. Contact the
state convention headquarters to determine which department can
supply materials or counsel in a specific area of concern.

These state Baptist agencies have materials available:
Christian Action Commission, Mississippi Baptist Convention Board,

Baptist Building, Jackson, Mississippi 39205.

Christian Life Commission, Baptist General Convention of Texas, Baptist Building, Dallas, Texas 75201.

Christian Life Council, Baptist State Convention of North Carolina, 301 Hillsborough Street, Raleigh, North Carolina 27611.

Cooperative Ministries: Christian Life, Kentucky Baptist Convention, Middletown, Kentucky 40243.

Department of Social Ministries, Baptist General Association of Virginia, Virginia Baptist Building, P. O. Box 8568, Richmond, Virginia 23226.

Other Resource Agencies

American Friends Service Committee, 160 N. 15th Street, Philadelphia, Pa. 19102.

Anti-Defamation League of B'nai B'rith, 315 Lexington Avenue, New York, N. Y. 10016.

Board of Church and Society of the United Methodist Church (Division of Peace and World Order, Division of Alcohol Problems and General Welfare, and Division of Human Relations and Economic Affairs), 100 Maryland Ave., N.E., Washington, D. C. 20002.

Center for Social Action, United Church of Christ, 297 Park Avenue, South, New York, N. Y. 10010.

Commission on Social Action of Reform Judaism, 838 5th Avenue, New York, N. Y. 10021.

Commission on Social Action, United Synagogue of America, 3080 Broadway, New York, N. Y. 10027.

Department of Church in Society, Division of Homeland Ministries, Disciples of Christ, P. O. Box 1986, Indianapolis, Ind. 46206.

National Association of Evangelicals, Social Action Commission, 1405 G Street, N.W., Washington, D. C. 20005.

National Council of Churches (Departments of Marriage and Family Life, Social Justice, Church and Economic Life), 475 Riverside Drive, New York, N. Y. 10027.

National Ministries/Social Ministries, American Baptist Churches, Valley Forge, Pa. 19481.

Office of Research and Analysis, The American Lutheran Church, 422 South Fifth Street, Minneapolis, Minn. 55415.

Unit on Church and Society, United Presbyterian Church in the U.S.A., 475 Riverside Drive, Room 1244 K, New York, N. Y. 10027.

U. S. Catholic Conference, 1312 Massachusetts Avenue, N.W., Washington, D. C. 20005.

Information on Specific Issues

Resources on specific social issues are quickly dated. Here are some suggestions, however, for securing up-to-date resources on social issues:

1. Write to the Christian Life Commission of the Southern Baptist Convention requesting information, bibliographies, materials on the issue you are concerned about.

2. Write to other organizations listed in the section on "Resource Organizations" in this chapter for general information.

3. Look in the card catalogue of the library and in the *Subject Guide to Books in Print* for a listing of available books on the issue.

4. From current magazines, newspapers, and periodicals maintain a file of materials on social issues.

5. Compile a list of organizations and their addresses which deal with specific issues. Such a list can be developed as you read books, magazines, and newspapers and attend conferences, classes, and meetings touching on social problems. The following is a sample of such a listing; it is not comprehensive and the viewpoints are not necessarily those of the author. But information from different points of view can be obtained from such agencies.

Family Life

American Social Health Association, 1740 Broadway, New York, N.Y. 10019.

Child Study Association of America/Wel-Met Inc., 50 Madison Avenue, New York, N. Y. 10010.

Children's Bureau, U. S. Department of Health, Education, and Welfare, 330 Independence Avenue, S.W., Washington, D. C. 20201.

Marriage and Family Life, National Council of Churches, 475 Riverside Drive, New York, N. Y. 10027.

Parents Without Partners, Inc., 7910 Woodmont Avenue, Suite 1000, Washington, D. C. 20014.

Public Affairs Pamphlets, 381 Park Avenue South, New York, N. Y.
10016.

Daily Work and Economics

Department of Church and Economic Life, National Council of
Churches, 475 Riverside Drive, New York, N. Y. 10027.

Economics Department, South Dakota State University, Brookings,
South Dakota 57006.

Joint Council on Economic Education, 1212 Avenue of the Americas,
New York, N. Y. 10036.

Race Relations

Civil Rights Division, U. S. Department of Justice, Constitution Avenue
and Tenth Street, N.W., Washington, D. C. 20530.

Commission on Religion and Race, National Council of Churches, 475
Riverside Drive, New York, N. Y. 10027.

National Association for the Advancement of Colored People, 1790
Broadway, New York, N. Y. 10019.

Southern Regional Council, Inc., 52 Fairlie Street, N.W., Atlanta, Georgia 30303.

U. S. Commission on Civil Rights, 1121 Vermont Avenue, N.W., Washington, D. C. 20425.

Citizenship

Baptist Joint Committee on Public Affairs, 200 Maryland Avenue, N.E.,
Washington, D. C. 20002.

Center for the Study of Democratic Institutions, Box 4068, Santa Bar-
bara, California 93103.

Council on Religion and International Affairs, 170 E. 64th Street, New
York, N. Y. 10021.

Democratic National Committee, 1625 Massachusetts Avenue, N.W.,
Washington, D. C. 20036.

The League of Women Voters, 1730 M Street, N.W., Washington,
D. C. 20036.

Republican National Committee, 310 First Street, S.E., Washington,
D. C. 20003.

Special Moral Concerns

American Medical Association, 535 N. Dearborn Street, Chicago, Ill. 60610.

American Social Health Association, 1740 Broadway, New York, N. Y. 10019.

Guidance Associates, 757 Third Avenue, New York, N. Y. 10017.

National Conference on Social Welfare, 22 W. Gay Street, Columbus, Ohio 43215.

United States Department of Health, Education, and Welfare, 330 Independence Avenue, S.W., Washington, D. C. 20201.

Christian Life Commission Resources

Materials Available from the Christian Life Commission of the Southern Baptist Convention

Cost of materials: All of the following materials sell for 5¢ per copy except where indicated otherwise. Write the Christian Life Commission for an order blank with an up-dated listing of materials. On cash orders add the following amounts for handling and delivery: $2 or less, add 25¢; $2.01 to $5, add 50¢; $5.01 to $10, add 75¢; over $10, add $1.00. Minimum order is $1.00. On charge orders, postage or shipping costs will be added to billing.

"Christian Life Style for Families" (fifteen in the series)
 Aging
 Communication
 Conflict
 Discipline
 Divorce
 Marriage Is for the Mature
 Marriage Outside Your Faith
 Moral Values in the Home
 One-Parent Families
 Parents and Teen-Agers
 Planned Parenthood
 Relation to Relatives
 Religion in the Home
 Roles in Marriage
 Working Wives and Mothers

"Christian Life Style for Youth" (six in the series)
  The Care and Feeding of Parents
  Fight Moral Pollution: Have Character
  Good News About Sex
  Marriage and What Your Mother Never Told You About It
  Please Keep Off the Grass . . . and H . . . and LSD . . . and
  What's Fun, Fantastic, and Christian? Dating

"Issues and Answers" (thirty in the series)

Abortion	Law, Order, & Justice
Aging	Mass Media
Alcohol	Open Housing
Black Power	Peace
Capital Punishment	Pollution
Civil Disobedience	Population Explosion
Communism	Pornography
Consumer Credit	Poverty
Drugs	Race Relations
Extremism	Revolution
Gambling	Sex Education
Generation Gap	Taxation
Guaranteed Income	Totalitarianism
Honesty	Urban Crisis
Juvenile Delinquency	Violence

"Christian Life Committee Guidelines" (A free pamphlet about the organizing and functioning of a Christian Life Committee.)

"The Christian Life Commission" (A free brochure about the history, purpose, and work of the Southern Baptist Christian Life Commission.)

"Interracial Marriage"

"What to Do About Pornography"

"Register Citizen Opinion" (Sells for 25¢ per copy. A list of all Senators and Congressmen, their addresses, and helps for writing them. Published annually.)

Proceedings from Christian Life Commission Seminars (Sell for $2.50 each. Published annually on such subjects as integrity, family, economics, national priorities, and citizenship.)

Selected Addresses from the Annual Christian Life Commission Seminars (A packet of six cassette tapes. Sells for $15 per set.) The following addresses are included:
  Kenneth Chafin—"The Relationship Between Authentic Evangelism and Authentic Morality"

John Claypool—"Communicating Moral Values Through the Uses of
Power Inside and Outside the Church"
President Lyndon Johnson—Two addresses to seminars
William H. Crook—"Christians Confront the Poverty Challenge"
Ramsey Clark—"Justice for All in a Discorded America"
George Kelsey—"Racism: The Special Problem of Christianity"
Eugene A. Nida—"Communicating the Gospel to a Revolutionary Age"
Samuel Miller: "The Christian Religion in a Technological Age"
Joseph Fletcher and Henlee Barnette debate—"The New Morality"
Anson Mount and William M. Pinson, Jr. debate—"The Playboy Philoso-
phy"

Suggested Programs
Objectives:

To strengthen Christians as they live the Christian life in the world;

To enable the church to fulfill its responsibility in the community
and in the world; and

To help create, with God's leadership and by his grace, the kind
of moral and social climate in which the church's witness for Christ
will be most effective.

1. Special Weeks
   A. Christian Life Week or Applied Christianity Week or The Bible
      and Life Week
      Sunday Morning
         Sunday School opening assemblies focus on Applied Christianity
         Sermon on Applying the Gospel
      Sunday Evening
         Training Union focus on Doing the Truth
         Evening service, Panel presentation on Public Morals
      Monday through Friday or Monday through Wednesday
         7:00 P.M.-7:55 P.M. Simultaneous seminars on Family, Race,
            Daily Work, Citizenship, and Special Moral Concerns
               (Leaders with special competence should be secured,
               study materials assembled, and church members pre-regis-
               tered for each seminar.)
         8:00 P.M.-8:45 P.M. Assemble for preaching

(It has been found that the same preacher on applied Christianity each evening generally maintains the greatest sustained interest. The seminar leaders, however, may share the preaching responsibilities.) Sermons may deal with Family, Race, Citizenship, Daily Work, and Special Moral Concerns.

Special features may include a breakfast meeting for men with an emphasis on "The Other Six Days," a dinner for leadership with an emphasis on "What It Means to Be a Christian" or "The Meaning of Church," a luncheon meeting for women on "Christian Liberation for Contemporary Women," and an after-service for young people with an emphasis on "Moral Decision Making."

B. Christian Family Life Week

Sunday Morning

Sunday School opening assemblies focus on Family Life

Morning church service to include a special testimony and sermon on "A Future for the Family"

Sunday Evening

Training Union focus on Christian Life Style for Families

Evening service, special speaker on "Your Home Can Be Christian" to be followed by dialogue with the congregation

Monday through Friday or Monday through Wednesday

6:00 P.M.-6:30 P.M. Church fellowship supper

6:45 P.M.-7:45 P.M. Simultaneous conferences on such topics as:

Boys and Girls in the Home

Preparation for Marriage

On Being Married (Young Marrieds)

Christians and Sexuality

Parents of Teenagers

Living with Parents (for Teenagers)

Conflict in the Home

Strengthening a Sound Marriage

Divorce and Parents Without Partners

Aging

7:50 P.M.-8:50 P.M. A sermon each night on some subject related to family concerns especially relevant to the church. Either the pastor or a visiting family life specialist, or experts in different fields may do the speaking.

Special features may also be arranged as suggested for the Christian Life Week.

(Excellent resource materials for Christian Family Life Weeks may be secured by writing to the Family Ministry Section, Church Administration Department, Baptist Sunday School Board, 127 Ninth Avenue, N., Nashville, Tennessee 37234.)

C. Christian Citizenship Week

Sunday Morning

Sunday School opening assemblies focus on biblical insights on Christian Citizenship

Morning church service to include special music related to citizenship and a sermon on "Christians *Are* Citizens"

Sunday Evening

Training Union to focus on Christians using political power

Evening church service to include both a special testimony from a Christian in politics and a sermon or panel presentation dealing with Christians and involvement in the political process

Monday through Friday or Monday through Wednesday

7:00 P.M.-7:50 P.M. Either the pastor or some other leader can teach the whole group each night or leaders can be enlisted to direct simultaneous conferences on:

Christians and Citizenship in Historical Perspective

What It Means to Be a Christian Citizen

Understanding How Government Functions

Christians Involved in Practical Politics

Guidelines for Christians in Political Action

8:00 P.M.-8:45 P.M. A message each night may be heard either from the pastor or from a visiting speaker or from specialists in such areas as practical politics, law enforcement, crime prevention, juvenile delinquency, religious liberty and separation of church and state, public education, and effecting social change.

A question-and-answer period afterward for about thirty minutes can be especially helpful on the subject of Christian citizenship.

Special features consisting of meals and dialogue between local political officials and interested church members may profitably be arranged during this week.

D. Crusade for Christian Morality Week

Using basic patterns suggested in preceding sample programs, the emphasis may be altered to deal with personal morality, honesty, sexual purity, pornography, gambling, alcohol and other drugs, violence, pollution, crime, profanity, war and peace, international affairs, or world issues.

E. Other Special Weeks

Important matters affecting the life and work of the church such as race relations, economics and daily work, church and state, or alcohol and other drugs may be highlighted as the need arises. Such topics may be dealt with in ways comparable to those previously suggested for applied Christianity in general, family, or citizenship.

2. Special Programs (Local church, associational meetings, student conferences, community programs)

A. Emphasis: Applying the Gospel

7:00 P.M.	Song and praise service
7:10	Scripture and prayer
7:15	Panel on "The Christian Life" (10 minutes each)
	Family Life
	Public Morals
	Race Relations
	Economic Life
	Citizenship
8:15	Song
	Special music
	Message, "Applied Christianity"

B. Emphasis: Mission Advance and Social Concern

10:00 A.M.	Worship in song
	In prayer for our missionaries

10:15	"Mission Advance Demands Christian Families"
10:40	"Mission Advance Demands Christian Action in Race Relations"
11:05	"Mission Advance Demands Christian Citizenship"
11:30	"Advancing Through Social Convictions"
12:00	Adjourn

C. Emphasis: Christian Citizenship

5:00 P.M.	Church council meeting or deacons meeting
6:00	Church supper
7:00	Song service
7:15	Scripture and prayer
7:25	"Contribution of Public Schools to Christian Citizenship"
7:45	"Separation of Church and State"
8:05	"Christian Citizenship and Law Enforcement"
8:30	Special music
	Sermon: "The Bible Speaks on Christian Citizenship"

D. Emphasis: Crusade for Christian Morality

7:00 P.M.	Song service
7:10	Scripture and prayer
7:15	"Honesty"
7:30	"Christian Citizenship"
7:45	"Personal Purity"
8:00	Song and special music
8:10	"Advancing Through Social Convictions"

E. Emphasis: Living the Christian Life

7:00 P.M.	Song service
7:15	Scripture and prayer
7:20	"Christian Life in Business"
7:30	"Christian Life in School"
7:40	"Christian Life in the Home"
7:50	Congregational song
7:55	Special music
8:00	Expository message: " Keep My Commandments"

F. Emphasis: Let's Take a Look at the Vital Moral Issues Facing Christians Today

9:55 A.M.	Special music
10:00	Scripture and prayer

10:05	Hymn
10:10	The Deceit of Beverage Alcohol
10:30	The Dangers in American Homes
10:50	Hymn
10:55	Desecration of the Lord's Day
11:20	Special music
11:30	The Demand for Church and State Separation
12:00	Fellowship luncheon

G. Emphasis: Christian Morality—A Twentieth-Century Imperative

10:00 A.M.	Hymn time
10:10	Scripture and prayer
10:15	Family Life
10:30	Christian Citizenship
10:45	Congregational Hymn
10:50	Juvenile Delinquency
11:05	Promotional period
11:20	Special music
11:30	Message: "The Divine Imperative"

H. Emphasis: Religion Is Relevant

7:30 P.M.	Song and praise service
7:45	Scripture reading (Romans 13) and Prayer
7:50	Special music
7:55	Panel presentation of "A Call to Relevance"
	(5 minutes each)
	Family Life
	Public Morals
	Race Relations
	Economic Life
	Christian Citizenship
8:20	Song
8:25	Special music
8:30	Message: "Relevant Religion"

An Annotated Bibliography of Books on the Practical Application of Christianity

The following books are recommended by the Christian Life Commission of the Southern Baptist Convention for use in church libraries. Without giving full approval of all that is said in all of the books that are listed here, it is felt that readers will find them helpful in gaining a better understanding of the practical nature of the Christian faith. The books are all in print and are arbitrarily, except for the General section and the section on Special Moral Concerns, limited to five titles in each section. Dewey decimal classifications are used.

General

Barnette, Henlee H.

> *Introducing Christian Ethics.* Broadman, 1961. $3.75. An introduction to Christian ethics in two parts, principles and problems. Biblical foundations for Christian ethical decisions are set forth and applied to major problems—the self, marriage and the family, race relations, economic life, and political life.
>
> 171.1 Christian Ethics/Bible—Ethics

DeWolf, L. Harold

> *Responsible Freedom: Guidelines for Christian Action.* Harper and Row, 1971. $10.00. This compact volume interweaves rules and norms with a discussion of real moral problems. It is a basic approach to understanding Christian ethics designed for the serious students of ethics.
>
> 241 Christian Ethics

Gardner, E. Clinton

> *Biblical Faith and Social Ethics.* Harper and Row, 1960. $7.50. This book majors on the Bible's teachings concerning Christian social ethics. It is widely used as a Christian ethics text in seminaries.
>
> 241 Christian Ethics

Kee, Howard C.

> *Making Ethical Decisions.* "Layman's Theological Library Series." Westminster, 1957. Paper, $1.00. This is a practical guidebook for understanding how moral decision making takes place.
>
> 171.1 Christian Ethics

MacQuarrie, John (ed.)

> *Dictionary of Christian Ethics.* Westminster, 1967. $7.50. Here is a valuable reference book which defines most significant terms used in the study of ethics. It contains many resource articles on social issues.
>
> 241.03 Christian Ethics—Dictionaries

Maston, T. B.

> *Biblical Ethics.* Word, 1969. $5.95. This is a valuable survey of biblical ethics in nontechnical language.
>
> 220.8 Bible—Ethics/Christian Ethics

Maston, T. B.

> *Christianity and World Issues.* Macmillan, 1957. $5.95. This resource and reference book relates Christianity to world crises and provides extremely thorough and well-documented perspectives on family, race, economics, political life, communism, and war.
>
> 261.8

Moberg, David O.

> *Inasmuch: Christian Responsibility in the Twentieth Century.* Eerdmans, 1965. Paper, $2.45. This is an especially helpful study of the Christian's social responsibility from a biblical point of view.
>
> 261.83 Sociology, Christian/Church and Social Problems

Family

Clinebell, Charlotte H., and Howard J., Jr.

> *The Intimate Marriage.* Harper and Row, 1970. $5.95. This book is written for married couples who want to strengthen their relationship by achieving deeper intimacy in a number of areas including sex, work, recreation, aesthetics, and family crises.
>
> 301.42 Marriage

Denton, Wallace

> *Family Problems and What to Do About Them.* Westminster, 1971. Paper, $2.85. Written by a perceptive marriage counselor and professor of family life, this book helps couples deal with everyday tensions and thus move toward deeper intimacy.
>
> 301.42 Marriage/Family

Duvall, Evelyn M.

> *Family Development.* Lippincott, 1967; 4th edition, 1971. $9.95. This comprehensive study discusses the developmental stages of family life.
>
> 301.42 Family

Mace, David R.

> *Whom God Hath Joined.* Westminster, 1953. $2.85. This book of

instruction and counsel can help young married couples achieve a better understanding of marriage as a Christian institution. It may be used before marriage and throughout married life.

301.426 Marriage

Trueblood, Elton, and Pauline

The Recovery of Family Life. Harper and Row, 1953. $2.95. This is an important, though brief and plain, call for Christians to give attention to building genuinely Christian homes.

392.3 Family

Race

Allport, Gordon W.

The Nature of Prejudice, 1954. $10.50. A comprehensive and systematic survey of group prejudice with an emphasis on the social, legal, and economic aspects of the problem. The author focuses on the deeper psychological causes of hatred and conflict.

157.3 Prejudices and Antipathies

Franklin, John H.

From Slavery to Freedom: A History of American Negroes. Random, 1969. Paper, $3.95. Here is a basic study of black history which gives essential information for an understanding of the contemporary racial situation.

325.2 Negroes—History/Slavery in the U.S.

Haselden, Kyle

The Racial Problem in Christian Perspective. Harper and Row, 1959. Paper, $2.25. This book examines the role of American churches in race relations, the nature of prejudice and how Christians may conquer it, and the religious basis for creative action in today's racial crisis.

261.83 Church and Race Problems/Race Problems

Knight, Walker L.

Struggle for Integrity. Word, 1969. $4.95. A moving account of the struggle of a Baptist church to minister in a racially mixed neighborhood.

286.175 Decatur, Ga. Oakhurst Baptist Church/Church and Social Problems/Church and Race Problems/Christian Social Ministries

Maston, Thomas B.
  The Bible and Race. Broadman, 1959. Paper 85¢. This is a brief, readable, widely used treatment of scriptural teachings related to race.
  280.832 Race/Human Relations/Sociology

Citizenship

Gaddy, C. Welton
  Profile of a Christian Citizen. Broadman, 1975. $1.95. The Christian citizen is characterized as a true believer, liberated servant, prophetic patriot, compassionate reformer, and prayerful participant. A primer for citizen action, found in the last chapter, can be helpful.
  261.7 Christianity and Politics/Citizenship

Green, Mark J.; Fallows, James M.; Zwick, David R.
  Who Runs Congress? Bantam Books, 1972. Paper, $1.95. An extremely helpful book aimed at aiding ordinary citizens to make their voices heard on Capitol Hill. The practical guidelines, personal references, and detailed illustrations of this "primer for citizenship" are very beneficial.
  328.73 U. S. Congress

Niebuhr, Reinhold
  Moral Man and Immoral Society. Scribner, 1932. Paper, $2.45. This is a scholarly treatment of individual and national morality pointing up the distinction between the behavior of individuals on the one hand and of social, national, racial, and economic groups on the other.
  301 Social Ethics/Political Ethics

United States Government Organization Manual (Government Printing Office, printed annually). Paper, $3.00. This is an invaluable resource book for concerned citizens.

Valentine, Foy
  Citizenship for Christians. Broadman, 1965. Paper, $1.50. A practical guide to understanding the biblical, historical, and political dimensions of Christian citizenship. The last section contains the basic documents of democracy.
  261.7 Christianity and Politics/Citizenship

Economics and Daily Work

Boggs, Wade H., Jr.

All Ye Who Labor. John Knox, 1961. Paper, 50¢. God's command to "subdue" the earth provides the theme for this book. The author traces the theme through the Bible and applies it practically to work, worship, and leisure in modern life.

248 Work

McLelland, Joseph C.

The Other Six Days. John Knox, 1961. Paper, $1.00. The author discusses the meaning of work and property, relating man's worship on Sunday to the other days of the week. The reader will likely disagree with some of the viewpoints of the author, though the book contains some helpful insights.

261.8 Christianity and Economics

Oldham, Joseph H.

Work in Modern Society. John Knox, 1961. Paper, 50¢. This book discusses work in today's world and seeks to help Christians to know and to do the will of God on the job.

179 Work

Redekop, John H. (ed.)

Labor Problems in Christian Perspective. Eerdmans, 1971. Paper, $6.95. This is a collection of essays exploring a variety of aspects of labor problems.

241 Work

Trueblood, Elton

Your Other Vocation. Harper and Row, 1952. $2.50. A most useful book calling Christians to live under Christ's lordship on the job and in all of life.

262.14 Christian Life/Church Work/Laity

Special Moral Concerns

Bainton, Roland H.

Christian Attitudes Toward War and Peace. Abingdon, 1960. Paper, $2.25. The writer traces the history of the various attitudes Christians have taken toward war—including pacifism, the "just war," and "holy war." He relates these to the atomic age.

261.63 War and Religion/War

Barnette, Henlee H.

Crucial Problems in Christian Perspective. Westminster, 1970. Paper, $2.45. Professor Barnette provides Christian guidelines here for such moral problems as drug addiction, alcoholism, gambling, highway safety, population explosion, racial prejudice, and capital punishment.

261.8 Church and Social Problems

Barnette, Henlee H.

The Drug Crisis and the Church. Westminster, 1971. Paper, $2.95. Here is a comprehensive treatment of drugs—including a discussion of types of drugs, an evaluation of the drug cult from a Christian perspective, and suggestions for rehabilitation.

362.293 Drugs/Narcotics

Haselden, Kyle

Morality and the Mass Media. Broadman, 1968. Paper, $2.50. After giving an excellent critique both of legalism and relativism, the author sets forth his understanding of biblical morality which he calls "authentic morality." Then he examines the relation of authentic morality to various issues related to mass media.

261.8 Church and Social Problems

Hollis, Harry N., Jr.

The Shoot 'Em Up Society. Broadman, 1974. Paper, $1.50. A critical review of the sources, dimensions, types, and future of violence in a "gore-nography" culture. Practical suggestions on what to do about violence complement careful analysis of the problem.

261.8 Church and Social Problems

Howell, John C.

Teaching About Sex: A Christian Approach. Broadman, 1967. $3.95. This book presents a practical, theologically sound study of sex education in the home and church.

241 Sex/Sex Instruction/Sexual Ethics

[Other recommended materials: (1) "Christian Sex Education: A Resource Packet." Broadman, 1971, $2.50. This packet includes a basic booklet on a Christian understanding of sexuality plus practical suggestions for sex education in the home and church. (2) A graded series of books, "Sexuality in Christian Living Series," published by Broadman in 1973.]

Maston, T. B., and William M. Pinson, Jr.

Right or Wrong? Revised Edition. Broadman, 1971. $3.50. The writers give practical help in making moral decisions in this Baptist best-seller. Particularly helpful for young people and those who work with them.

284 Christian Ethics

Rust, Eric C.

Nature: Garden or Desert. Word, 1971. $4.95. This ecological study is based on theology and science. It offers a sound Christian foundation for action to save the environment.

230 Nature (Theology)

Conclusion

No single church can do everything that is suggested here. But every single church can—and should—do something. For a church to do nothing in social action is not to remain neutral. It is to contribute to the evil which mangles human life. Can a person claim innocence if he remains neutral while a murderer conducts his gory business? Can a church remain guiltless if it keeps silent in the midst of racism and oppression? To say "no" to social action is to turn society over to godless persons. To remain silent in the face of injustice is to condone it. Christian social action is a required course of action for a church true to God's will.

Because social action is right does not mean it is easy, however. Application of the gospel is difficult. It may be the most demanding aspect of a church's ministry. There are few easy victories and perhaps no perfect ones. That's not surprising. Since even the death of the Son of God for our sins did not immediately usher in a perfect society, we can be sure our human efforts will fall short. Although perfection may not be possible, certain progress is. If he is persistent, the Christian with God's help can help improve the world. Persistence is important. In spite of defeats, frustrations, and antagonism, churches must keep trying.

A Christian life apart from social action is a shadow of the best God has for his children. Without application of faith to life, the Christian witness is bland. Accepting God's call to be the salt of the earth and the light of the world brings life in its fullest. Striving to see God's will done on earth as it is in heaven—that's an exciting challenge. The church committed to changing the world won't be a boring fellowship. Everyday will bring new opportunities to bear witness by applying faith to life. Hopefully this book will help your church experience that kind of meaningful life.